Decolonising
Multilingualis

WRITING WITHOUT BORDERS

Writing Without Borders exists to provide space for writing and thought which challenges the norms of academic discourse. Books in the series will touch on Multilingual Matters' key themes – multilingualism, social justice and the benefits of diversity and dialogue – but need not focus entirely on them. Books should be short (20,000–40,000 words is ideal) and represent a departure in some way from what and how you would usually write a journal paper or book manuscript. They may contain experimental writing, new ways of thinking or creating knowledge, topics that are not generally addressed in academic writing, or something we haven't thought of yet.... The series is a place to explore, think, challenge and create. If you are not sure if your idea is 'right' for this series, please ask us.

Writers from the Global South will be particularly welcomed and sought out, as well as writers from marginalised communities and groups within the Global North. Writers from all academic disciplines are welcome, as are experts working in non-academic settings.

Full details of all the books in this series and of all our other publications can be found on http://www.multilingual-matters. com, or by writing to Multilingual Matters, St Nicholas House, 31–34 High Street, Bristol BS1 2AW, UK.

WRITING WITHOUT BORDERS: 1

Decolonising Multilingualism

Struggles to Decreate

Alison Phipps

MULTILINGUAL MATTERS
Bristol • Blue Ridge Summit

DOI https://doi.org/10.21832/PHIPPS4054
Library of Congress Cataloging in Publication Data
A catalog record for this book is available from the Library of Congress.
Names: Phipps, Alison M., author.
Title: Decolonising Multilingualism: Struggles to Decreate/Alison Phipps.
Other titles: Decolonizing Multilingualism
Description: Blue Ridge Summit: Multilingual Matters, [2019] | Series: Writing
    Without Borders: 1 | Includes bibliographical references and index.
Identifiers: LCCN 2018060943 (print) | LCCN 2019010418 (ebook) |
    ISBN 9781788924061 (pdf) | ISBN 9781788924078 (epub) |
    ISBN 9781788924085 (Kindle) | ISBN 9781788924054 (hbk : alk. paper) |
    ISBN 9781788924047 (pbk: alk. paper)
Subjects: LCSH: Imperialism and philology. | Decolonization–Social aspects.
Classification: LCC P41 (ebook) | LCC P41 .P45 2019 (print) | DDC 306.44/6–
    dc23
LC record available at https://lccn.loc.gov/2018060943

British Library Cataloguing in Publication Data
A catalogue entry for this book is available from the British Library.

ISBN-13: 978-1-78892-405-4 (hbk)
ISBN-13: 978-1-78892-404-7 (pbk)

Multilingual Matters
UK: St Nicholas House, 31-34 High Street, Bristol BS1 2AW, UK.
USA: NBN, Blue Ridge Summit, PA, USA.

Website: www.multilingual-matters.com
Twitter: Multi_Ling_Mat
Facebook: https://www.facebook.com/multilingualmatters
Blog: www.channelviewpublications.wordpress.com

The policy of Multilingual Matters/Channel View Publications is to use papers
that are natural, renewable and recyclable products, made from wood grown in
sustainable forests. In the manufacturing process of our books, and to further
support our policy, preference is given to printers that have FSC and PEFC
Chain of Custody certification. The FSC and/or PEFC logos will appear on
those books where full certification has been granted to the printer concerned.

Typeset by in Sabon and Frutiger by R. J. Footring Ltd, Derby, UK
Printed and bound in the UK by the CPI Books Group.
Printed and bound in the US by Thomson-Shore, Inc.

Contents

Acknowledgements   vii
Introduction   1
A Short Manifesto for Decolonising Multilingualism   5
    If We Are Going To Do This…   5
    Obedience   12
    Gifts Are in the Feet   16

Part 1: Decolonising the Multilingual Body   17
 1 Deep Pain Is Language-Destroying   19
    If You Say My Name   21
    White Mask   25
 2 More Than One Voice   26

Part 2: Decolonising the Multilingual Heart   31
    The Gist   31
 3 Hospitality – Well Come   33
 4 Attending to the Gist   39
    Folding a River   44
 5 Waiting   46
 6 Waiting Brides   49
 7 Waiting Bodies   56
 8 Screens   60
 9 Parting Gifts   66
10 Muted and Hyphenated   68
Coda: Gifts Are in the Painted Feet   70

Part 3: Decolonising the Multilingual Mind   71
11 *Chitsva Chiri Mutsoka* – 'Gifts Are in the Feet'   73
    The Land   74
    Aroha   77

12	*Mihi*	80
13	*Te Reo* – The Māori Language	82
	Can You Hear My River?	86
14	Conclusions	89
	Gifts Are in the Feet	89
	Disobedience	93
References		95
Index		98

Poem titles shown in italic

Acknowledgements

This book is made by many people, all authors of the experiences, the conversations and the languages I have encountered. It's authored by those who brought into being some of the most effectively brutal structures of oppression known to education – those against the grain of which I have struggled. Without these structures of rendering invisible, inaudible the languages of authors, within pedagogical structures, this book would not have come to be. This book owes a debt, therefore, to its foes.

Far greater is the debt to its friends.

Without the administrative care of Lauren Roberts and Bella Hoogeveen the work could not have been undertaken. All the following were part of the gestation and witnessing to this work: Gameli Tordzro, Naa Densua Tordzro, Tawona Sitholé, Julien Danero, Robert Gibb, Prue Homes, Mariam Attia, Jane Andrews, Richard Fay, Sarah Craig, Karin Zwaan, Chantelle Warner, David Gramling, Ross White, Obed Kasule, Rosco Kasujja, Maria Grazia Imperiale, Giovanna Fassetta, Judith Reynolds, Melissa Chaplin, Lyn Ma, Katja Frimberger, Charles Forsdick, Kofi Agykum, Kofi Anyidoho, Nazmi Al Masri, Sophie Nock, Chaz Doherty, Piki Diamond, Jabaru, Nii Tete Yartey and the Noyam Institute for African Dance, the Glasgow Refugee, Asylum and Migration Network, Seeds of Thought; The Iona Community. Rami and Kirsty at Blair Atholl Watermill, for wifi and all manner of good things.

The many invitations to offer plenary and keynote lectures have led to both new experiences and the opportunity to perform, air and interrupt the work and the poetry. These were generously provided by University of Glasgow; Keele University; Stirling University; King's College, University of London; the Centre for Contemporary Arts, Glasgow; Glasgow Centre for Population

Health; Glasgow School of Art; University of Arizona; Islamic University of Gaza; University College London; Cologne University; Te Whaiti School, Te Urewera; University of Waikato; Auckland University of Technology; University of Auckland; University of South Australia; University of Melbourne; Victoria University Wellington; University of Victoria, British Columbia; Buenos Aires Museum of Immigration; University of London; Hong Kong Polytechnic University; British University Dubai; University of Otago; University of Western Australia; St John's Fremantle; Maryhill Integration Network; Calais Refugee Camps; Cities in sub-Saharan Africa; Noyam Institute for African Dance, University of Ghana, Legon; Dublin City University; University College Cork, United Nations Conference on Languages, New York; Solas Festival, Scotland.

Special thanks to Piki Diamond, Sophie Nock, Gameli Tordzro and Tawona Sitholé for offering vital comments during the gestation of the manuscript. And a particular debt is owed to David Gramling, Ross White and Charles Forsdick for their reading of the full draft and administering of the kind of comments which teach you as you work, and illuminate the dark corners, by bringing a smile to the task of editing.

The work was funded with the support of the Arts and Humanities Research Council Translating Cultures Large Grant: Researching Multilingually at the Borders of Language, the Body, Law and the State. AHRC Grant Ref: AH/L006936/1. To all at Multilingual Matters, especially Anna Roderick, my humble thanks for your willingness to risk, and your patience with my frailties.

For those who remained at home with their love as I travelled, wrote, made and spirited forth the work – Robert, Rima – words for sufficient gratitude fail me – as they should.

Alison Phipps, UNESCO Chair for Refugee Integration through Languages and the Arts at the University of Glasgow.

Arts & Humanities
Research Council

Titiro, Whakarongo … korero.

Look, listen … speak.

Introduction

This short book begins from the premise that multilingualism and its attendant language pedagogies are largely experienced as a colonial practice for many of the world's populations. It takes as its starting point N'gugi Wa Thiong'o's view that the imposition of colonial languages on Africa, and by extension many countries across the globe, inhibited communication and the carriage of culture for those whose languages were sliced up by the lines drawn by the colonisers (N'gugi Wa, 1986). One way in which this slicing occurred, and continues to be made manifest, is in the language pedagogies of the global north.

How languages are learned and taught, the political economy of the organisation of language curricula and language policies favour the world's colonial and imperial languages – English, Spanish, French, Chinese, Russian, Portuguese and to a lesser extent Italian and German. Through specific conceptions of multilingualism and language pedagogy a raft of peace-building, interpreting, intercultural dialoguing policies have been attempted, largely serving Western democracies, but these have remained radically impervious to the languages which have not been part of the colonial projects. To be sure, there have been attempts to shore up local, community and indigenous languages, especially in some of these Western democracies, but it is true that many languages remain on lists of those critically endangered or extinct. Metaphors of ecocide have strikingly been applied to this linguistic situation (Phillipson, 1992; Skutnabb-Kangas, 2000) and have replaced those previously used for the study of language – of kinship and family resemblance.

Much academic ink has been spilled on the subject of declining numbers of languages and rates of language learning, other than historically dominant languages. English language pedagogy is a multi-million pound industry, and the linguistic imperialism and risks this causes are well documented (Canagarajah, 1999; Phillipson, 1992; Skutnabb-Kangas, 2000). The responses in recent years have come from renewed understandings of multi-lingualism and more recently of translingual practice – a waking up, it seems, in the West, to the fact that most of the world's speakers have a wide variety of language repertoires (Blackledge & Creese, 2010; Cameron, 2013; Canagarajah, 2013; Gramling, 2016; Moore, 2015).

At the same time there is much masking of the role that languages might play in the processes of decolonising which have emerged from postcolonial legacies, and in resistance to the homogenising cultural effects of globalisation. A case in point is the *Handbook of Critical and Indigenous Methodologies* (Denzin *et al.*, 2008) – a genuinely wonderful resource and attempt to bridge two important political and academic fields, but in which there are no index entries to either multilingualism or to language(s). The volume is chock full of essays presenting the perspectives of indigenous peoples the world over, where the medium is, for the most part, English. At times, especially, and notably, in the chapters by Māori scholars, *te reo* is present, as it is in the speech of everyday life in Aotearoa New Zealand. Sometimes indigenous idioms are used or particular concepts are rendered in their original form, but for the most part, in the rich and engaging essays, and critical resilience, language is merely a vehicle, or is perceived as a barrier, never as a means with which to decolonise, or to experience the process, from the global north, of what decolonising might require in terms of discomfort, pain, commitment to methodological awkwardness, hesitancy, to a lack of control, transparency and fluency (Jones & Jenkins, 2008).

The current book offers a series of autoethnographic narra-tives, fragments, poems, interludes, critical reflections and some theoretical engagement. It begins, subjectively, from my own attempts at grappling with not so much the theory, as with the lived, felt practice of decolonising and my realisation that my own multilingualism, with which and for which I had toiled with a fiercely resistant pride, was simply that of one who is fluent in way too many colonial languages.[1] Mbembé (2000) describes the task of trying to reach a point where we, in the Western traditions, can experience otherness as follows:

> We should first remind ourselves that, as a general rule, the experience of the Other, or the problem of the 'I' of others and of human beings we perceive as foreign to us, has almost always posed virtually insurmountable difficulties to the Western philosophical and political tradition. (Mbembé, 2000: 2)

There is an important point to be made from the outset. Criticism can rightly or wrongly be levelled at my decision to write and publish on the subject of decolonising. There is an important argument for getting out of the way and allowing those who see themselves strictly as colonised and marginalised subjects to undertake this work and not for more white feminists or postcolonialist or critical scholars of any kind to take up space, but instead to make room. I'm fully aware of these calls and of the subtle and not-so-subtle politics of strict identity which accompany them. I am indeed perceived to belong to and now function within a class with certain types of privilege, not least as someone drawing a salary at a university which prizes its global rankings. There are forces which shaped me over which I had no control, and others over which I can now, and do exercise choice. Each of those choices requires me to give an account of myself, and this offering is another opportunity for doing just that (Butler, 2005).

The argument that white, imperialist, Anglo-hegemonic projects have done quite enough damage and the best moral approach is to just stop taking up space is one I can understand. There is a parallel strand in feminism which requires power to be shared, and ceded, for new constellations of equalities to emerge. But the colonial project did not discriminate in its many colonisations of minds. The imperial mindset, schoolings, legacies are still alive and well today and writ large in new forms. The task of trying to live out their decolonisation as a critical, phenomenological project belongs in corridors of power, such as the academy, and it needs a multiplicity of narratives of the vulnerability in resistance which form such projects (Butler, 2016).

At every challenge and turn, the question of whether to speak or step back is one negotiated between the many requirements placed on me by my employer and the requirements placed on me by those seeking asylum or establishing new lives. There is no pure place to stand, and as I heed both call and critique, on balance, those critiquing my attempts to decolonise are in the main white, highly educated and Anglophone, and those calling me to do more are not. There are many different judgements to be made about what to do with your privilege: own it; use it; pass it on; pass on it; make space; and many other arts which need a lifetime of struggle, apology, reparation and some mutual celebration, which can hint at a post-decolonial world.

The lived, felt practice I describe and reflect with here comes from 'leaning in' to indigenous contexts and being reconstituted dialogically, with those seeking asylum and refuge, as well as relationally with those living under siege or occupation. It represents what Raymond Williams terms 'creative practice' (Williams, 1977) – an attempt to break with colonial, epistemic ways of seeing in order to open a space for a way of writing between philosophical prose, personal story and poetic activism. As such, it has been 'a struggle at the roots of the mind', a participation, and a decreating commitment (Weil, 2002).

Note

(1) Helene Grøn is responsible for this wonderful formulation, in email correspondence.

A Short Manifesto for Decolonising Multilingualism

If We Are Going To Do This…

> If we are going to do this, if we are going to decolonise multilingualism, let's do it as an attempt at a way of doing it.

The only way to decolonise is to do it. It needs some forethought but ultimately it needs actions which are redolent with decolonising attempts, adding to critical learnings of previous decolonising attempts. It needs people who are able to embark on such a journey and return with tales to tell of what happens when decolonising is attempted in foreign languages learning. The tales are messy, compromised and always within what Spivak calls the 'double bind' (Spivak, 2012), a place within which there will always be dis-ease and a sense of not having reached a resolution. A place which, in critical terms, will always be found wanting, bearing traces of that which it wishes to divest.

> If we are going to do this, let's cite with an eye to decolonising, citing from the global South, giving multilingual scholars much more airtime than usually accorded, alongside more women, who are the ones tasked with the teaching and interpreting of languages for the majority of the world's population, through the mother languages.

But let's not just do that. Let's also cite from indigenous peoples who know all about the loss of land and language; and from the displaced peoples – the refugees, asylum seekers and diaspora who are now placed in the frontier spaces where transactions of bodies, words, beliefs are dissolving the known world. And let's do this all with an eye to those fluent-in-too-many-colonial-languages aspects, which are part of the critical context, and double bind of all multilingual working which I have been formally educated into to date. And where there is no hope of the *scholare* which affords material relief such that thinking, reading and writing might be achievable (Bourdieu, 2000). Let's stop pretending our ways of knowing, our epistemologies, are the only valid ways of knowing something. Let's work harder to cite those who live and work in languages other than English, or at least other than English first. The experts by experience, where experience is often carried through generations, have much that is stored in the scars and the skin, and to know in these ways means taking a journey away from books and firewall-protected double-blind peer-reviewed articles in top-ranked journals.

So, readers, this short book will not just cite all the usual suspects all over again – I respect their work greatly and many are working as I am, in elitist, top-100 universities, cycling the canonical white English language texts between students and conferences, masking the multilingual by the requirements of clarity, cohesion, transparency and an academic publishing world of words which keeps on putting English first, and then putting those first whom the counters find to have the most citations, in English. And that is not a decolonial practice. It's quite the opposite. And it administers more colonial metrics.

> If we are going to do this, let's not only cite with references to publications.

Words – black against a white page – are part of the flattened out hegemony of a text-based literacy within which the spoken word is so deprived of oxygen that it cannot live and there can be no pedagogy of the art of the vocal or what Freire describes as 'pronuciar o mundo' – pronouncing the world (Freire, 2006). There is a different power to the spoken word, a solidarity with the oral and performing arts which have long been the places where indigenous and precarious knowledge has been stored, memorised and shared. There is a protocol which is followed in the folk tradition whereby storytellers, poets, musicians tell from whom they learned a thing, an ancestry which respects the fact that none of us ever create a single word without our mothers, grandmothers, our elders and teachers and the sounds all around us.

> If we are going to do this, then we need to rethink our copyright and intellectual property claims.

It remains a lived reality that property is theft, not least in the eyes of indigenous and colonised peoples. 'Accept theft or die' is N'gugi Wa Thiong'o's call (N'gugi Wa Thiong'o, 1986). We need models of a creative commons and of stewardship, of the return of land and of language to common care from the sites of bureaucratic control, standardisation and curricularised codifications. Such sites of control serve those wishing to deploy human capital, not those striving to care for the persistent diversity of human life, and human languages and the myriad forms their sharing and learning may take. A language cannot be owned; nor can its teaching. It is the first sharing that occurs in human life between the child and parent, the first whispered words of hospitality. These are the places a serious decolonising attempt of multilingualism will need to explore to stand any chance of finding a way out of those insurmountable difficulties notions of property have caused within the Western philosophical and epistemological traditions.

> If we are going to do this, then let's improvise and devise. This is how we might learn the arts of decolonising.

We aren't going to get it right first time. Or even the tenth time. It's not something you can clean up theoretically or conceptually and have a correct methodological framework for developing. It's going to be messy, it's going to be like all creative human endeavour, it's going to need some awkward practice, uneasy rehearsals, the development together of new scripts which we trace out from having made it up as we went along the journey with others. And it is not about knowing lots, but about particularities and granularities of experience. The colonised cannot know decolonisation in the same way as the coloniser, but as with all experiences of violence there are some structural similarities to the ways in which the damage to both will manifest. Colonisation works within the framings of trauma and decolonising will work in the nooks and crannies of unstable behaviours, memories, numbness and vivid recall. A similar description is found in Ijeoma Oluo's descriptions of tackling racism (Oluo, 2018). Unlearning habits of oppression and inequality is not straightforward or neat and tidy. And this should not be an excuse for inaction. It will mean sometimes language is where we relive those violences and struggle with their ongoing effects, as we try to use them in recovery (Costa & Dewaele, 2014).

If we are going to do this, then we need different companions.

We might need to be allies, perhaps, but I'd prefer co-conspirers, in that wonderful sense buried in the etymology – '< French *conspire-r* (15th cent. in Littré) (= Provençal *cospirar*, Spanish *conspirar*, Italian *conspirare*), < Latin *conspīrāre* lit. "to breathe together", whence, "to accord, harmonize, agree, combine or unite in a purpose, plot mischief together secretly"' (*Oxford English Dictionary*). The idea of allies – as with ideas of perpetrator and victim, of coloniser and colonised – always draws thick lines where porosity exists. It's vital that privilege and position are part of our ongoing reflection on where we speak from and on behalf of whom, but it's not the end or even the beginning of the story. In conspiring, we have a sense of participation in a collective, porous endeavour, not of stepping out of the world in whose suffering, loss and oppression we are so implicated, nor by believing we have the answers and expertise to clean up that very mess. Autonomy is an important principle in this work, but the mess we have made, of peoples, land, languages, rivers and the air, is no respecter of nationally drawn postcolonial boundaries and any decolonising foreign language learning endeavour worth its salt will need to remember the intimate connections between land, language and its need of the air for speech, any speech, anywhere, to find articulation.

It was not only Bakhtin who understood that we are made through dialogue with others; we are permeable beings, in his dialogic imagination, with transindividual subjectivities. This logic is at the heart of *ubuntu* understandings, which have been widely posited as a counterbalance to the Cartesian dualisms of individual mind and individual body, which allowed the kinds of abstractions and divisions to take form which are intrinsic to the colonial and neo-colonial logics. *Umntu ngumtu ngaabantu* – 'a person is made by other people' – is the Xhosa expression, pointing to a transindividuality, and dialogic constitution and change wrought by those with whom one speaks. It follows that the way in which this dialogue is constituted – in Bakhtinian terms – its diglossia and heteroglossia – will be part of the material formation of ever-changing subjectivities.

An intentional decolonial multilingualism will need to pay attention to who, and in which terms, quite literally, it is in dialogue. If that dialogue is constituted only in Anglo-normal or all too colonial linguistic and discursive terms, then some work will need to be on the cards.

> If we are going to do this, we will need artists and poetic activists to break the hold of the discourse of the colonising multilingualisms and foreign language pedagogies and their performative assumptions.

Struggles need their fools, the Lords of Misrule, the place of the carnevalesque, the people who start out on a crazy journey, looking and sounding very unlike the mainstream, weaving their words in daring ways which are poetic and different and without doubt often foolish enough to be dangerous to all that is normative and believing in its own parameters. Mary Carol Combs wrote a wonderful piece about 'goofiness' in language teaching (Combs, 2014). Speaking words which change the dull echo-chambers of the soundscape; speaking words which are not a backing track but which will be heard. It's part of the co-conspiring work. And poetry remains, according to the Welsh poet writing from within what he understood as colonial conditions, 'that which enters the intellect, by way of the heart' (R.S. Thomas).

> If we are going to do this, let's do it in a way which is as local as it is global; which affirms the granulations of the way peoples name their worlds.

In this wee book I insist on my own local geographies, my kinships with places as their own genealogies of experience and decolonisation. Colonialism is about a particular violent set of practices and knowledges, which insert themselves into and write over particular local contexts. So, naming the small places, the townships and abodes, the places where dwellings have been made and lives are lived out, often a long way from the centres of decision-making power, but where decisions are made to retain local naming practices – these matter to the decolonising task. I speak in this book of Camas, of Iona, of St Porchaire, of Whirinaki, Biberach an der Riss, Dodowa. These are places in which a vernacular persists and with their own ways of pronouncing their place in the order of things which has a defiance and a resistance when spoken by visitors. They are often unassuming places but their retention of local names with their own meanings requires a respect of them with the decolonising journey. But this is not simply about localisms, but rather the way the patterning of this can be found globally to resist, subsist, struggle on, or to die away but be retained and returned in fragments of oral narrative and story.

> Finally, if we are going to do this, let's do it multilingually, let's language it.

For the last few years I've been holding the threads, as a leader, of the at times technocratic, at times intellectually stretching, at times creatively glorious space in which a large, multi-million pound grant project – Researching Multilingually at the Borders of Language, the Body, Law and the State – has been attempting to decolonise various academic disciplines and methodologies. It is a complex project which has taken place with refugees and displaced or oppressed peoples worldwide and in a range of conflict zones, with researchers working, and mostly failing to work, multilingually in their academic practice – both individually and collectively, across a range of elite and grassroots multilingualism. From our trials and errors and moments of bright breakthrough have come the beginnings of both a creative practice for researching multilingually, and theorisation of what this might mean methodologically, critically and ontologically.

From the devising of online siege-breaking Arabic curricula in the Gaza Strip to the refugee detention centres of Bulgaria, from the appeal courts for asylum claims in Europe to the recovery attempts of child soldiers in Uganda, to the dance performances of Dangbe young people in Ghana, researchers have worked with diaspora arts from former British colonies to make attempts at decolonising language methodologies and pedagogies. The multilingual attempts have failed as much as they have succeeded in cracking open a space where we might begin in the mother tongues of all who are present and allow ourselves to make a way for our work, multilingually, deliberately shirking the pull to a single language for ease of administration. Interestingly, the multilingual attempts which have most succeeded are those which have been least engaged with the learning of other colonial languages.

And in this, let there be no 'us', except as an imaginative, *ubuntu* force. For it is vital to recall that to decolonise has to be a process of learning with and through difference and that the hope for an arrival at a common, collective place of understanding is to deny the necessity of constant difference. Those moments of connection can only be fleeting, made in ceremony and performance and ritual events, but not enduring, for this moment in history. The imagination can hold out for a unity, a oneness, as I have found repeated time and again in the autoethnographic experiences I describe here from participant observations. But structural inequalities cannot be overcome in a research project or even in a family set of relationships. They endure and must be endured, as part of the disquieting and enduring dis-ease of all activism that is at the heart of all critical and decolonising work.

Obedience

I spent the day in obedience
Unwriting all that has been written.
Unwalking the beech strewn paths.
Unthinking all that has been thought
Unfeeling all sensuous sensation.
I let the water lap around my skin
then unlapping, let the water join the mist.
I held only air.
Spoke only with silence.
Touched only where the shadows lay.
I reeled in every prayer, unhooked the bait,
Threw the fish back into the water.

Decreated I surveyed the battlefield.

Warriors are not warriors outwith wartime.
Warriors are gardeners, poets,
spirits of the living,
spirits at one
with the dead.

Decreated, I tore the many words from my lips,
the many thoughts from my mind,
the hopes from my heart.

Decreated I left the dance floor.

And for a while
my land had rest from war.

Alison Phipps, 2018

This short book offers a critical and autoethnographic glimpse into some of the learning which has come from the decolonising attempts and the many errors and lessons involved in trying to decolonise language learning and multilingualism. In it, I situate myself in a variety of roles, but primarily as a language non-knower in situations where the normal power relations of language are reversed. I do so by taking at face value the critical injunctions to write in such a way as to unsettle the arrogance of ignorance derived from institutional authority which can often lead to the fragmentation of bodies of knowledge. Such fragmentation gives rise to a misguided elitism which, in turn, creates tensions and contradictions between theory and practice.

Often theorists devalue practice whereas practitioners dismiss theory as unnecessary and cumbersome while not realising that there is always a theory that explains practice, acknowledged or not. And in both, the light and shade of languaged experiences are masked.

I deliberately work with defamiliarising, hyper-local and poetically, rhetorical strategies which can throw the reader into a critical stance or puzzlement – what does that mean? Where is that? I've never been there? I've not heard of that? This is an attempt to unsettle and allow a world to be brought into view, which is not framed in the usual Englishes, or through recourse to the usual centres of power or canonical authors. This is poetic work trying to offer countervailing examples to the prevailing spirit of neo-colonialism, of 'upscaling' and homogeneity. In his essay *The Redress of Poetry* Seamus Heaney reflects that:

> in the activity of poetry too, there is a tendency to place a counter-reality in the scales – a reality which may be only imagined but which nevertheless has weight because it is imagined within the gravitational pull of the actual and can therefore hold its own and balance out against the historical situation. (Heaney, 1995: 3–4)

Heaney's understanding draws directly on Simone Weil's *Gravity and Grace*, where she writes:

> If we know in what way society is unbalanced, we must do what we can to add weight to the light scale … we must have formed a conception of equilibrium and be ever ready to change sides like justice, 'that fugitive from the camp of conquerors'. (Weil, 2002: 171)

It is in this vein of redress, of equilibrium, that I offer this as an attempt at multilingual justice. An attempt. A struggle to decreate.

I have also chosen to adopt the set of working principles outlined above to guide the work, attempting to enact a critical narrative but also to entice the reader into dialogue through a decolonising foreign language journey I have undergone myself as part of the larger project I outline above.

While this journey has been undertaken in many different contexts – in my own home with those seeking refuge, in detention centres, in classrooms, on remote Scottish Islands, in the Gaza Strip, the Arizona desert, the rainforest of the Dangbe people – I specifically chose here to draw on the lessons I have learned from indigenous people and those seeking or waiting for refuge with whom I have come into relationships, work and patterns of life which have required me to struggle, to unlearn and to decreate.

In Part 1, I look at the lessons learned from injury, from the use of my own vulnerability and pain, a starting point for resisting certain forms of knowledge, and practice. In Part 2, I consider a different linguistic vulnerability and wound, created in the light of and despite my many colonial multilingual fluencies, that of the lack of my daughter's tongue, as her foster mother. Finally, in Part 3, I consider the language lessons, in particular from Sophie Nock (Nock, 2005; Nock & Crombie, 2009) and through her teaching and my learning of *te reo*, the Māori language, and decolonial methodologies from Piki Diamond and Chaz Doherty (see Buissink *et al.*, 2017) and from Linda Smith (Tuhiwai Smith, 2012) in the context of the bicultural decolonising processes underway in Aotearoa New Zealand.

I end with the example of Aotearoa. While far from perfect and in many ways just taking its first hesitant steps, the work of biculturalism in Aotearoa, and of mutual decolonisation between Pākehā and Māori, has already brought new, creative forms of process and possibility into being. The political settlements made in both *te reo* and in English show how conceiving of justice and dialogue multilingually requires an expansion of thought, a hospitality to words, a decreation of all the practices which have been forged linguistically and destroyed rights of land and livelihood across generations (Durie, 1998).

In *Te Kawa o Te Urewera* (Te Urewera Board, 2017), a work of poetic, human ecological policy-making and philosophy for such decolonising and decreative work, the newly recognised legal personality of Te Urewera, the land, is the central focus, upon her return to the stewardship by Tūhoe, as another example of *ubuntu*, transindividual dialogical thinking, affect and action.

This disconnection from the land is the primary violence of settler colonialism, cultural, technocratic and linguistic

Image from *Te Kawa o Te Urewera* (Te Urewera Board, 2017: 8, 23)

colonialism. The erasure of languages under the pressures for coherence, transparency, efficiency and control; the primacy of reaction and curation all threaten diversity. The multilingualisms, admirable as they may be, of the Common European Framework of Reference have not addressed the structural imbalances and precarity of situation of those whose loss of land has also meant erosion of the space through which languages were cultivated (Gramling, 2016). Language revitalisation is a long road, and rather like the work of refugee integration policies, it requires diverse, transversal actors and critical engagement.

This short book is an attempt to offer an example, not from within the global south but within the academy of the north, an example of solidarity and hope, which is far from naïve. It offers an answer to those critics who may see as naïve and unattainable the fond hope I hold for a shifting away from the all too colonial language legacies in our Western schooling, towards ecologies of neighbourliness, dialogue and decreation. It's a step. That's all. But others are walking this way too, just not in the places where we have been most accustomed to tread.

For this reason, I chose to embark on this decolonising story by also breaking into my own prose, with poetry, with the spoken-word lessons of the elders, and with gifts in the feet.

Gifts Are in the Feet

You say 'the gifts are the feet'.
It is wartime.
So shall I walk away
Shall I flee to the hills
Cross the seas
Ford the rivers
In spate?

If I wear out
My shoes
Will the ache fade
Will the longing
Recede
Will I stand at last
Somewhere on the heart's
Edge
And sing
Again.

Of love.

I say the gifts are in the tears
I say that salt and water
Show what needs
To flow.
I say stay with the river
On your face,
Feet on the battle ground
Gifts come from the grieving earth
Watered with the
Longing in my eyes.

Alison Phipps, 2018

Part 1: Decolonising the Multilingual Body

With Naa Densua Tordzro, Gameli Tordzro, Jabaru and the Noyam Institute for African Dance, Dodowa, Ghana

1 Deep Pain Is Language-Destroying

A healer has my ankle firmly in his grasp and is drawing his thumb and index finger down over the swellings, along the nerve endings, where the blood circulates, pushing the fluid away to allow for repair. I have never known pain like it. My consciousness comes and goes. I scream out. Next to me a trusted companion has my hand in her tight grip. I bite into the cloth, which covers my head, and writhe in agony. My breath comes in gasps. I have lost my ability to speak. There is no sense to be made of the world, just a reaching of the limits between pain, voice and the darkness of a mind slipping its moorings. All language has left me, and I am only able to scream. My companion begins to sing. I cannot understand her words, but the rhythm and pattern of her breath tell me that this is a song that will accompany pain. As she breathes, I breathe. As my consciousness wanes, her singing intensifies.

Spivak speaks of double binds (Spivak, 2012), drawing on Bateson, and here is one of my own: I'm leading a dance production project as part of Arts and Humanities Research Council research into multilingual idioms of distress, wellbeing and resilience, and I am discovering the limits of my pain threshold, in the process of being healed.

Under a full moon, on a warm, light night in Accra, I slipped off a kerb stone as I was saying farewell to a colleague, and the at once familiar, agonising, nausea-inducing crunch and shock of pain told me that I had, once again, ripped the anterior ligaments in my ankle – a severe sprain – and that there would be no dancing for me for months to come. I immediately followed the first-aid training I'd received: RICE – Rest it, Ice it, Compress and Elevate. The swelling and bruising began to appear quickly. In between reassuring my research team that I would be 'fine', I began to consider what to do practically to make sure our work could continue. We were going to need to engage our driver more fully, and a second driver too. We phoned our regular driver, a trusted favourite within our project work. His response was surprising, and in Ewe. 'Yes, of course I can do more driving for you, but I can also work on the ankle, the traditional way'. Then he paused before saying slowly, 'But it will be painful'.

We discussed his offer. It was unlikely to do harm, and reducing the swelling would perhaps help with the healing. I was certainly prepared to try pretty much anything, as I was aware that what I'd done I'd done before, and it would be at least eight weeks before I was mobile again and three before I could put weight on my foot. Shortly after the call, our driver arrived and began to inspect the damage carefully and with a trained eye. Next to me I could hear the gentle translation from my colleague. There were nods and shakes of the head, and then the offer was made again: 'But it will be pain-full.' He was not sugar-coating it.

> Intense pain is also language-destroying: as the content of one's world disintegrates, so that which would express and project the self is robbed of its source and its subject. Word, self and voice are lost, or nearly lost. (Scarry, 1985: 35)

This moment of hearing the words 'pain-full' became a visceral and pivotal post-decolonial moment, a moment of decision to trust what Western epistemologies of medicine did not appear to counsel, or, more accurately, to represent. The idea that deepening pain would relieve and heal more intensely was counterintuitive to the therapeutic, consumer paradigms of medicine in the West. It was an ethical moment of decision in the middle of the double bind, the profound irony of attempting to lead a dance project in Ghana on one leg, when I could not walk, let alone be part of the physicality of directing a production. It was a moment when my white skin marked me fully as someone who would not be at all likely to respect the traditional wisdom being offered by a multilingual, subaltern taxi driver. In a project dealing with idioms of distress and resilience, collecting the traditions held in multilingual proverbial wisdom and storytelling, this was a moment of symbolic and political decision too.

> The authentically political, […] arises out of a commitment to thought in a certain mode, thought aware of its own production, its own vulnerability and its own commitment to risk. (Williams, 2007: 68)

As the description above makes clear, I accepted the offer of healing. It was not to be a monetary transaction, on any account. This was contrary to the tradition and protocols. And I was to be accompanied, witnessed to, by my two hosts and colleagues, during the twice-daily treatment.

'I am ready,' I said. Willing.

Before the first session took place, our driver – my healer – washed his hands and, after checking he had my permission, for the third time, took shea butter and coated his own hands first and then began to coat my foot. And after that, I do not know what his art was, as I could not concentrate on anything other than enduring, containing and breaking with the pain. All I could see were the orange-black lights of pain stars. I lost vision. I lost speech. I lost some consciousness. All I could do to help myself was scream.

If You Say My Name

Gifts are in the feet.
They bring your voice to my ear.

Tears are in the hair,
Your hand helps them
rise up through my breath.

War wounds abound
and strength is here
abundantly.

But if you say my name
the world of death
where I stand on a shoreline
with the drowned,

Where I kneel in the smoking
rubble with the bombed.

If you say my name
where I shake, barefoot, on the shards of glass
scattered across the bedroom

Where I listen in to the words
which wound with accusation,
disappointment,
blame and anxiety.

If you say my name
when the letter comes,
and the key turns and the decision falls
and she is taken away.

If you say my name
As you said her name
In the garden, after the battle,
after death was done
and after war wounds
were wrapped in balm and cloth.

If you say my name.
Gifts are in the feet.
If you say my name.
Tears are in the hair.
War wounds abundantly.
If you say my name.
Say my name.

Alison Phipps, 2018

The four of us fused, during these ritual moments of treatment, structured socially and interculturally, in ways which resemble those the anthropologist Clifford Geertz describes in 'Deep Play: Notes on a Balinese Cockfight'. In his narrative of attending the third match of a cockfight in Bali, not long after his arrival, he describes how the police and army roared up to the event, and 'only slightly less instantaneously' than did his hosts, he too – as part of what he describes as the 'superorganism' of the crowd – ran with the dispersing crowd (Geertz, 1973: 415).

The point Geertz notes in his narrative is that once the police began questioning his hosts in the yard to which the crowd had dispersed, his hosts leapt to his defence, in a sign of clear acceptance. 'The next morning the village was a completely different world for us,' he said, with everyone knowing the story of how he 'had fled like everyone else'. For Geertz, in his description and analysis, this is because of the cultural shift he had undergone by following the cultural instincts of the crowd, and 'siding' with their practices, thus also rendering everyone safer.

My own situation was slightly different. A superorganism was also formed, with the rhythm of the healer-driver's hands on the skin and bone and nerve endings of my foot, and my witnessing colleagues beginning to breathe alongside me as the expression of physical pain writhed from my body in cries. They spoke for me, breathed with me, the healer-driver never once slackening his expert movements, but softly saying 'sorry, sorry, sorry-o, sorry-o'. But it was certainly true that immediately after the first treatment the relationships were completely different. Once the haze of pain had lifted, and my breath recovered enough for me first to laugh, and then to breathe out deeply, and then to speak, I could stand, and I could walk, reasonably evenly.

There is a part of this story which is interesting for the extent to which this treatment accelerated the healing of my foot. Treatment sessions twice daily meant that within 10 days I was doing what would otherwise have taken nearly eight weeks from previous experience of the same injury. But this is not what interests me here in this reflection on decolonising multilingualism. What this moment, rather like Geertz's recounting of the Balinese cock fight, shows me is that something substantial has to be risked, some threshold has to be crossed into something which is not knowable, until one is over on the other side, and speech/language/breath has to be risked at the same time for decolonising to happen, however temporary it may be.

Decolonising is, indeed, the changing of the relationships of power, control and dependency into ones where there can be a shift towards an equality that was not possible under the previous arrangements. It may well be that many of the hierarchies are still intact afterwards, and that the categories of race, gender and class are still doing their work within the structures of social relations, but the fact of these relations having been 'in solution', as Williams (1977) describes it, means that simultaneously a new set of relations come into being.

There were hierarchies between us: a white English-speaking professor, leading a research project in Ghana, a project in international development and multilingual learning, and the black Twi-Ewe-, Akan-, Hausa-speaking driver, employed for the duration of the project. These relations relied on certain social protocols, ways of greeting one another, ways of placing my own body and his, forms of respect between guest and host, employer and employee. There were many things he knew about driving the streets of Accra which were mystifying to me, many words he would use in everyday speech I did not understand. These aspects of a respectful relationship between professionals functioned well, with moments of humour when I would attempt to use one of his many languages – but that was as far as it went, I think.

These had been the comfortable points of inversion we'd experienced in our work together on projects in the past, but the inversions brought by my handing over of my injury to his treatment enacted a different transformation altogether. And fundamentally it was not so much about experiencing new limits to pain and thresholds of pain in my body as about surrendering my power of speech and allowing it to fuse with that of the 'superorganism' of those witnessing and treating the injury. Decolonising was occurring as a decreation of the ability of the body to do anything more than scream. Word, self and voice were lost, and the previously colonially, or postcolonially, held relationships between us changed, fundamentally. The decolonising of multilingualism was a decolonising of language learned, yes, but more than that, it was a decolonising of the ability to produce or learn language at all, and a need for others to speak for me, and bring ease.

It would be naïve to think that all the power relations between a driver in precarious employment in Ghana and a white, middle-class professor in a reasonably secure tenure vanished. But it would be equally naïve to hold to the theory of change which suggests that it is only with a change at the societal or political level that decolonising can occur. Alison Jones and Kuni Jenkins write of this relationship as hyphenated, where the hyphen can never, and should never, be erased, and will be disquieting, uncomfortable and even downright agonising at times (Jones & Jenkins, 2008). In 2014 I published an article on intercultural methods entitled 'They are Bombing Now'. In it I called for critical vigilance and asked whether, as researchers, we are willing 'to go anywhere near the structural violence which holds inequality in place' (Phipps, 2014: 112).

What this agonising episode of pain and surrender of Western constructions of knowledge demonstrated to me, through my participation in the trusted knowledge practices of the context where I was a guest, was that when language dissolves in pain, new relations form around that pain, around its inflicting and its assuaging. Many hands and voices were joined around this moment, where both I and the healer were in the centre of the language fields.

The permeability of the body in pain, the way trans-individuality could form through the membrane of the bruising skin and the rushing of blood down the vein, has parallels with the massaging of my skin with olive oil after the hennaing by an older woman, or the way many hands dressed me as a Blen woman, which form the focus of Part 2 of this book. Both represent acts of integrating, here focusing on the decreating, disintegrating body. How such permeability endures will depend on our next meeting, and is a different and empirical question.

White Mask

Your gaze strips the skin from my flesh,
flesh from my bone
And the bones lie bleaching.

It's time to crack me open.
The marrow is still warm.

Blood-black.
Unmasked.
Ripe for the taking.

In this war.

Alison Phipps, 2018

2 More Than One Voice

In *For More Than One Voice,* Adriana Caverero (2005) challenges the roots of Western epistemology and metaphysics by critiquing the tradition of understanding Aristotle's notion of 'logos' in the *Politics* as equating to 'reason' or to the life of the mind, and, rather, drawing on the *Poetics* situates logos as spoken word, as the human-speaking-animal. To be human is to speak (phonetics) and meaning is interpreted from that speech (semantics) in the social sphere. When 'word, self or voice are lost or nearly lost' as Scarry (1985: 35) describes it, the fabric of the social is torn, and a 'superorganism' forms to enact repair – be it Amnesty International letter writers, or the driver-healer witness-colleague nexus which came together around my own minor injury.

Decolonising, then, is fundamentally about changing the human relationships of power around speech and language. To decolonise multilingualism is ultimately to decreate the speaking animal body of the human animal. It is not merely an epistemological task. When Mbembé (2000) describes the 'I' of the 'other' as posing 'virtually insurmountable problems to Western epistemology', it is perhaps this aspect of decreation he is grasping towards. The language of the coloniser and its pedagogical scaffolds, historically and in the globalising present, have to be stripped back to the human-animal, out of, prior to and outside of language.

What Cavarero is arguing is that the voice, the sonorous speaking animal, is presymbolic: it precedes interpretation and the lending of meaning to an utterance; it precedes words and works with sounds. Colonialism has come, in part, from the way in which certain modalities of speech, and 'human-speaking-animals' have been ignored as unintelligible – as unworthy, for the most part, of learning or recording by any but the most dedicated of missionaries (in order to convert), or anthropologists (in order to assign meaning) or occasional traders (in order to extract value). Colonialism has come from the way certain languages are not grievable, to use Butler's term (Butler, 2009).

The voice is that which 'precedes, generates, and exceeds verbal communication', an expression of 'reciprocal invocation' founded in 'the sonorous, rhythmic, and resonant materiality of the voice, [...] a duet, through which individuals mutually invoke one another' (Burgess & Murray, 2006: 29–30).

Cavarero shifts attention from what is being said to who is speaking, drawing on Arendt, 'to find a politics that recognises the singularity of each human life *before* [my emphasis] the human becomes an abstract category, an identity whose meaning relies on language' (quoted in Burgess & Murray, 2006). Burgess and Murray (2006), in their review of *For More Than One Voice*, critique the genealogical logic of a politics which relies on the cry of an infant and the response of the good mother, but where it is unclear how the response of the 'good mother translates to political relations between strangers'. The question as to how this relational duet is formed must therefore look to relationships and their formations under conditions which involve strangers, or at the very least people who are not cast in the role of the 'good mother'.

This brings me to consider the experience of treatment for a sprained ankle, in a context where I did not easily share language, was trying to learn languages and where I was in the hands of hosts who were stripping me of language, my own mother language included. These conditions placed me back into the presymbolic, into a place where 'Word, self and voice are lost' under pain and pressure. These moments lead us out of the politics of identity, or the logics of economics, and into new constellations of social and cultural relations. They are marked by the presence of the 'superorganism', by the presence of risk, by exigencies of the breath and the body, by loss of speech and by a shift in the power relations which dominate everyday life, often rendering the new constellations as permanent a feature as those which pre-exist, and enabling the creation of new scenes, upon which superorganisms come into being.

> Both [black people and white people] must turn their backs
> on the inhuman voices which were those of their respective
> ancestors in order that authentic communication be possible.
> Before it can adopt a positive voice, freedom requires an effort
> at disalienation. (Fanon, 1965: 180)

Both Fanon and N'gugi Wa Thiong'o, as early pioneers of
decolonising the mind, saw language retention and linguistic
resistance as vital to the task. Their writings show how the early
decolonising struggle did its courageous work and their part
in it. For N'gugi Wa Thiong'o, this work is characterised as a
'rediscovery of the real language of humankind: the language
of struggle'.

> The future of the African novel is then dependent on a willing
> writer (ready to invest time and talent in African languages),
> a willing translator (ready to invest time and talent in the art
> of translating from one African language to another); a willing
> publisher (ready to invest time and money) or a progressive
> state which would overhaul the current neo-colonial linguistic
> policies and tackle the national question in a democratic
> manner; and finally, and most importantly, a willing and
> widening readership. (N'gugi Wa Thiong'o, 1986: 108)

The colonising structures of language pedagogy have been
imposed, adopted, replicated across the world and it is far too
simplistic to see these as belonging simply in boxes marked
'perpetrator colonialists' and 'resisting colonised'. Freire (1970)
has shown clearly how struggles are bound up together and such
binary divisions merely replicate violating structures themselves.
What is described above for the African novel is true for all
cultural practices and everyday life. Those who decolonise are
those who practise decolonising; those who are *willing*. Their
starting points may be different, depending on their ancestry
and their heritage in imperial and colonial practices, but what
matters is the will to 'disalienation', to decolonise mind, heart,
body, and thus, consequently, to risk decreation.

What I have sketched here have been my attempts at doing
precisely this with my own multilingualism. These have been my
attempts at being willing to risk decreation by trying language

routes offered by those who, consciously or not, suffer the in-dignities of colonial language pedagogical practices, and where the marks of this are found in everyday life. Language can be a refuge, a shelter house and a home, but only if it is itself given refuge, shelter and home, most especially when under attack, or forced, in the bodies of its speakers, into exile.

The refugee, as Arendt reminds us, poses an ontological question: 'Refugees expelled from one country to the next represent the avant-garde of their people' (Arendt, 1943: 119). Agamben elaborates Arendt's sense, further seeing the figure of the refugee as constituting a 'radical crisis' challenging the idea of the nation state and of the rights of man, and of the citizen (1943: 116): 'That bare life [the human creature] […] now takes centre stage' argues Agamben and from this undeconstructable, bare life creatureliness 'perforates' the 'spaces of states' (1943: 119).

As those seeking refuge, and those whose languages have been colonised and reduced nearly to extinction, come into the consciousness of Western philosophising, once again, they continue to represent an avant-garde and a radical crisis to language pedagogy. Translanguaging, multilingualism point up the inadequacy of the state-bound, colonial legacies of language pedagogies and of the globalising policies of TEFL and ESOL. The nation states of the global North are beginning to come face to face with this bare life. Their responses are both hospitable and also hostile. Either way, the bare lives and the resistances before them offer a chance for the development of co-created, post-decolonial ways of learning.

In the work of the 'Researching Multilingually at Borders' project, we ended with a will to work entirely multilingually, with English last, or, as David Gramling (2016) puts this, 'in the caboose', with all the mother languages of the performers coming before. English came but just not in the vanguard, not as the avant-garde, and the results were astonishing. A post-decolonial multilingualism was willed into being, struggled over and turned into a dance production, expressing itself, first of all, through the movements of the singing bodies of Dangbe young people in a rainforest. And that is another story, for a different book.

Part 2: Decolonising the Multilingual Heart

The Gist

With the Waiting Ones
who we cannot yet name,
for fear.
Where they are now,
I do not know.
I must not know.
Until I know.

Alison Phipps, 2018

3 Hospitality – Well Come

Along the landing and into the apartment block is a trail of red rose petals and tiny tealight candles leading into a room with one huge bed. At the end of the line of lights and petals are the words, spelled out in rose petals too, 'Well Come'. Travel-weary as we are, not least from using airlines and operators which fly into majority refugee hosting contexts, and standing in queues for visa forms and visas, and complying with varieties of copycat bureaucratic process designed to mimic Western ways, it will still be 4am before the joyous celebrations of arrival end and we can fall into bed. As we enter the apartment the camera phones are already recording the moment, the endless kissing of cheeks and holding of arms, shoulders, hair, cheeks, the repeated, repeated, repeated greetings of peace – how are you? Selam, Selam, Peace – how are you? Peace, Selam, Peace – how are you? And then that is it, for the English. I'm over the threshold and the languages now are Tigrinya and Blen.

A young man met us with a small minibus at the airport. 'When I first knew him he had a rickshaw; now he has been here long enough to have a van', says a member of the family. My body is already everyone's property. In the minibus the women who met us hold my arms, my knee, my face, patting me repeatedly. My skin belongs to their care now. We do not share many words and so touch and smiles and nods are going to bind us through the time we are spending physically together. This is not going to be a time when 'personal space' is maintained and organised for in the way it is 'back home'. We are going to be living in close quarters and on top of each other, by any measures.

It's beautiful – the petals, the scarves fluttering, the colours telling of who we are with and where they belong, the candle light, bringing us to a place made as a home, welcoming.

One of the world's largest refugee groups since the early 2000s has been Eritreans seeking sanctuary. A totalitarian state run by a dictator – Isaias Afwerki – who has never called the elections required by its constitution and who operates a policy of enforced indefinite conscription to the army for men and women from 12th grade – so around 15 – until age 50. 'There are no young people in my country any more', says one of my hosts to me. No one is allowed to leave the country unless they are in their fifties and so, – by Eritrean life expectancy standards – old.

Says an old man:

If you are over 70 in Eritrea, they will not treat you if you go to seek medical help. They say – you can eat, that is enough for you.

Especially over the last 15 years or so, people have crossed the dangerous borders out of Eritrea into Sudan or Ethiopia and then they have tried to move north, west, south, even east over the Gulf of Aden into the Gulf states. Their stories of transit are marked by smuggling, trafficking, torture, extortion, slave auctions, imprisonment, by years spent lying low and living low, by days, months, years of waiting. And then the quieter stories, of help from friends, neighbours, strangers, gifts of food, shelter, money, transit refuges on the way. Until recently, if they made it to the Mediterranean, then it's the familiar story of sinking boats, coast guard rescue, then passing through Malta, Lampedusa, Sicily, Italy or, more recently, Lesbos, Greece.

It used to be that travel north from the Mediterranean countries was possible to an extent, depending on the Dublin II and Dublin III legal arrangements whereby someone seeking asylum has to remain in the country where they make their claim, disproportionately leading to the majority of Eritreans ending up in Italy and Greece over several years. Those who evade finger-printing after chaotic registration processes or arrival by boat may try to move north through Europe, to wherever they can get to, but mostly to try to get to someone they know, for safety's sake. And that normally means family, though for unaccompanied minors it may mean the cohort of other minors with whom they are placed in temporary holding accommodation en route or by social services.

We sit around a table groaning with food and are offered water. It's hot, and yet the apartment has a fan and intermittent air conditioning. Mostly, it's the electricity that's intermittent. At the airport there was a stand full of planes marked as 'United Nations'. It's not long before the conversation turns political, in the sense of what has to be done to survive daily. I have just enough mind-holds for meaning, scraps of language which will allow me to follow the gist and tone which come along in the conversation. I have just enough to praise the food and drink, to speak of family and to say that we are well, or to say that we are suffering.

The majority of the world's refugee populations do not live in camps, though it's hard to believe this given the persistent iconography of refugee camps, not least in refugee policy-making. Most of the aesthetic and imaginative energy surrounding both research and public discourse on refugees presents refugees as victims – half drowned, actually drowned, in tents, wretched, huddled human misery begging at the doors of the West. In refugee studies and advocacy too, there is a countering of this narrative with one of agency and resilience. The refugees who arrive in northern Europe are indeed the ones who have survived, often because they have access to the kinds of resources of family, wealth and education which can afford them connections and a degree of safety for the risky journeys. The majority of the world's refugees live in cities. Big cities in so-called 'third countries' soak up the transiting flows of people like huge bandages, as if staunching the blood from their countries of origin.

While the political, academic and media focus is on the richer countries around the Mediterranean, dealing largely with the specific flows of refugees from Syria – to Jordan, Turkey, Lebanon and, exceptionally, Germany – it has been business as usual in countries like Kenya, Uganda, Sudan and Ethiopia, at least for East Africa. Similar patterns persist in West of Africa too, and the vast majority of Afghan refugees, of course, are living in parts of Pakistan.

South–south migrations make up the vast majority of displacements of people across the globe. The numbers of those who actually make it North are tiny and the corridors of migration criss-crossing the global South are also unmarked, unlike those highly marked cases of the so-called 'hot-spots' in the North. The development of the 'hot-spot' metaphor as a way of marking a so-called crisis, a crisis of reception, in the global North continues the use of militaristic metaphors, such as 'strategy', 'tactic', 'target', 'management', and it has spawned a plethora of security and militarisation responses along the borders between the global North and South, notably between

Mexico and the USA; Europe and North Africa; Europe and Asia; South Asia and Australia. Elsewhere, people on the move are a normal part of life in large cities into which people migrate and flee and stay or move on again as conditions permit. Much of this, in the global South, is unremarkable and certainly little remarked upon, as attention is focused by the world's richest countries on their fear for their property.

For days now, as I float in a diaphanous gown around the apartment, unseen by the outside world, careful to stay behind windows barred or shuttered as much against prying eyes as against the scorching sun, people come in and out, knocking first, then entering. 'Ahhh, this is X's cousin, mother, grandmother, daughter.... This is my grandfather's brother's son, this is .... this is....' I cannot hope to hold any of the names easily in my mind, but what I do know is that this is the social security system for refugees living in this city in East Africa.

It's a lovely re-creation of the kinds of neighbourly ways of living I've heard told of from life 'back home' in Eritrea, though hidden away in an apartment block of Eritrean refugees, all of whom are waiting. I make meaning from walls, bars, air and arriving bodies, greeting me, meeting me, stroking my skin. All of this is backdrop against which the gist is gathered.

4 Attending to the Gist

Gist

(1) *Law*. The real ground or point (of an action, indictment, etc.).

(2) The substance or pith of a matter, the essence or main part. (*Oxford English Dictionary*)

To get the gist of something is to understand something of what is said, although not everything, but to get enough, as the definitions above suggest, for the essence to be grasped. Getting the gist of something is usually dismissed in favour of transparency, clarity, full comprehension as the goals of meaning, yet getting the gist is vital to communication and to translation. It is a vital constituent in the activities of language pedagogy, a way of adding, slowly, to the stock of words or phrases which are repeated and understood until there is a lexicon sufficient for getting the gist, and then getting more than the gist, and then, as if a fog is lifting, gradually, to realise you've been gist-getting for long enough for understanding to have come to be. How this happens has been laid out in many an applied linguistics study where the measures and frameworks for levels of language competency are detailed for assessors of language learning. What is absent from such work, however, is the subjective, autoethnographic reflection on the process of learning through which the gist is indeed to be got.

In my previous work I've worked authoethnographically as a participant- observer in language pedagogy, akin to what Kramsch calls 'the Multilingual Subject' (Kramsch, 2009). I've documented the experience of learning languages in language classes for community education, after hours, on the margins, with hourly paid teachers on precarious contracts. In a paper reflecting on linguistic incompetence as a methodological and ethical value (Phipps, 2013), I returned to my field notes from participant observation and identified several phenomena which are part of the experience and struggle against non-communication. Those field notes were from work in contexts of siege and occupation, and from among those with whom I lived and worked who were seeking refuge. The precarity of language pedagogy after hours, on the margins, with hourly paid staff, but not for purposes of leisure and learning languages with strong pedagogical resources – Italian, Portuguese – gave way to a whole new experience of language learning: one of struggling for the gist, outwith familiar pedagogical structures and resources, and with no, or highly limited, aids for learning the languages surrounding me (Phipps, 2007).

That paper identified similarities between the kinds of observations in early anthropologists' writings, especially Evans-Pritchard and Malinowski, and my own notes when I was unable to understand language in various settings where I was undertaking fieldwork – whether by way of English or through interpreters. In that paper I noted, retrospectively, that my field notes focused on rituals, clothing, food, objects, greetings and farewells, not on meaning, or or on language other than the words I was tentatively learning. I also noted how long it takes (around two years with intense concentration, good materials and attentive teaching) to learn a language sufficiently well to be able to overcome the first facet of the twofold problem of language (Ricoeur, 2007), the dilemma of 'translation from one language to another and translation internal to some spoken language'.

Ricoeur's second understanding of the problem of translation describes translation as a phenomenon which is 'greatly enlarged' when that problem is understood in the following terms: 'everywhere there is the foreign, there is a place for a struggle against non-communication' (Ricoeur, 2007: 23). The gist represents a kernel in this struggle against non-communication, and it manifests itself in contexts not of professional and translational ease, of a sharing of multiple languages relatively evenly between people, but rather in places where there is little or no equality in this struggle against non-communication. This he sees as not so much a question of the incommensurability of languages or the impossibility of translation, but one of justice vis-à-vis the threat of vulnerability inherent in simply not understanding what is being said – the vulnerability of a child before entry into language.

> This threat is more precisely inscribed among the figures of incapacity that affect our capacity to speak and, step-by-step, to say, to recount, up to and including moral imputability. (Ricoeur, 2007: 24)

How, when we do not share language, do we work at this fragile edge between human beings, those whose language dominates and those whose language is almost inaudible in cognitive terms? How do we show ourselves to be capable of speech, of presence in conversation and the social bond, how do we make and tell stories, and how do we create a space for ethics, without a language to share, or without a language in which to be understood as doing precisely this?

These questions inform the reflections throughout Part 2, where I am returning to my autoethnographic and subjective experience of vulnerability, even threat, in the context of my own refugee family. Their situation in life and that of others is one of much greater precarity than my own, and yet 'struggle against non-communication' as an active, exhausting performance of my own body reveals ways in which this experience works as well as a decolonising multilingualism, and as a methodological trajectory. This is the kind of place where people laugh out loud when you suggest you may wish to learn their language, or when you try to say some words, or when you point at objects and ask for the word in Tigrinya or Blen. It's a context where hardly anything which may resemble language pedagogy, such as is written of or researched by applied linguistics and in foreign language studies, is in existence. Its very absence is, *a priori*, decolonising. It forces a confrontation with all the privileged, literacy-rich, resource-intensive ways in which my own many colonial languages have been not simply learned, but refined, and learned for refined, elite endeavours.

The last remaining university in Eritrea, the University of Asmara, was closed in 2003 and there has been no higher-education capacity since then. There are barely any resources for learning Eritrea's nine official languages, with Tigrinya perhaps the best served in that there are some primers, an occasional course at the School of African and Oriental Studies in London and another, so the internet tells me, at Bowling Green State University, equally occasional. Given its particular history of being colonised, Eritrea has not been in a position materially or politically to develop resources which would vouchsafe its linguistic heritage in ways which would make its languages accessible to learners from outwith cultural norms. Eritreans seeking refuge cannot imagine that *Tsada* – fair-skinned Europeans – could possibly be interested in learning their language, even if people enjoy my interest and see it as a compliment to their way of life. This is not least because of the enormous emphasis placed on English language acquisition as part of integration politics in Anglophone countries of arrival. This is not to say that contexts for learning do not exist, but that what they look like, and how to discover them, are, to paraphrase Mbembé's observation (Mbembé, 2000) once again, almost impenetrable to the Western mind, searching as it does in its formal institutions, or in its own peculiar forms of autodidacticism, for knowledge.

The reflections which follow move between explanatory contextualisation, which is vital for the gist, and participant observations around my own body, dress, heat, hunger, thirst and skin, and the ways I was made at home with those wishing to move from indefinite waiting to seeking asylum.

The combination of my own incompetence, lack of language-learning resources in any way familiar to me, the lack of either interpreters or people willing to spend vital, energised and joyful time translating, left me in a position where observation was a default role, and participation was based on gist and gesture and objects which could be used to communicate. In consideration of decolonising, this is important, not so much for what is learned, but for what happens when context and knowledge are combined with the experience of being linguistically incompetent and with no clear sense of what to do about this – no phrase books, or dictionaries, or willing interpreters around. Language-learning and meaning-making come together from the knowledge of this context and language which swirls and forms and falls around what is already known, and the desire to understand.

For this, the gist is vital, and the gist is what I have used to frame and narrate these partial fragments. They stand as testimony to what can be known without a language, and from sensory observations primarily, but they also show that as part of decolonising language learning, incompetence and the opacity of knowledge must be lived and struggled with and even embraced, so that power imbalances can be experienced viscerally. Meanwhile, those with conventionally marginalised linguistic power, who routinely must make all their meaning in dominant languages in refuge arrival contexts through gist and through the good offices of others, can be themselves linguistically dominant. We can then experience why it is that, to quote Mbembé:

> We should first remind ourselves that, as a general rule, the experience of the Other, or the problem of the 'I' of others and of human beings we perceive as foreign to us, has almost always posed virtually insurmountable difficulties to the Western philosophical and political tradition. (Mbembé, 2000: 2)

Being able to get only the gist is indeed a virtually insurmountable difficulty for the Western philosophical and political tradition. In my own experience, it goes well beyond the idea of 'decolonising the mind'. It is not simply a cognitive exercise but more an act of what Anne Carson (2006) calls decreation, following Simone Weil (2002):

> Decreation: to make something created pass into the uncreated. Destruction: to make something created pass into nothingness. (Weil, 2002: 32)

By making something created pass into the uncreated, Weil argues, 'we participate in the creation of the world by decreating ourselves' (Weil, 2002: 33). This is not an act of cognition, but rather an ontological prerequisite of co-creating something new. This new co-creation, made with the world, not by the self alone, Weil sees as requiring an act of exile from the self, in order for decreation to be achieved, for that which has been created – the oppression and colonisation – to be uncreated.

> It is necessary to uproot oneself. To cut down the tree and make of it a cross, and then to carry it every day. It is necessary not to be 'myself', still less to be 'ourselves'.[...] We must take the feeling of being at home into exile. We must be rooted in the absence of a place. (Weil, 2002: 39)

It is within the lived experienced of my ever uprooting family of exiles, and my lived experience of handing myself into their care, that I've come to understand the felt sense and importance of ontological decreation, or what I'd like to call 'decolonising the heart'. Metaphorically, the heart is where the transindividuality of family and kinship takes its seat, at least in the Western imagination. It is the seat of the emotions. It breaks when those loved suffer or are absent. Having very little language at all that we might share means tearing from the self the eloquence which allows for power, presentation and performance, and which sustain and perpetuate domination. The muted vulnerability of such a position becomes a means of resisting the perpetuation of domination systems, whereby something other is experienced. Academic theorising struggles to grasp this, not least because it relies on dominant languages – this language in particular, which is here in front of you. But in the resistant vulnerabilities of affect (Butler *et al.*, 2016), and a risking of my own self in these permeable spaces which are so hard to reach in language, there is perhaps a chance of presenting what decolonising the heart, what ontological decreation, might entail.

Folding a River

When words have no place
in the plenty or the
empty
of what is
and what has been.

The currents twist
and the eddies defy
and the clear depths disguise
and the rocks conceal
and the trees stroke

the water's skin
not knowing where
to begin.

The river,
newly awake
begs for shelter.

mafuku.

It is wartime.

In the forest
after the storm
the river is born
in the trees.

mhango.

In her hands –
the streams of life drawn
from a clear spring
high up
on the
rocky moor.

guvi.

She drinks
and the river folds itself
into her belly
months before it is born,
its story to come,
but not yet, not yet.

Time for the telling
lies downstream.
Beyond the waterfall not seen
and the waves
on a far-off neglected shore.

Here in the *ruware*
it is time for the three
waters of the source
to hide in her bone breast,
granted fragile protection
from all that may be
said
or told
too soon.

Alison Phipps, 2018

5　Waiting

A good deal of attention is paid to what it means to live in limbo in the UK while awaiting decisions on immigration. During this waiting time there is little (perhaps £36.50 a week) or no financial support from the state. Over the last 15 years I have been alongside and then within families where waiting for a decision, which will mean that a normal life can be lived again, has become a normal part of my own life. 'I am waiting for my papers', 'I am waiting to be released from detention', 'I am waiting for my bail hearing', 'I am waiting for my housing', 'I am waiting for my interview', 'I am waiting for a decision', 'I am waiting for my lawyer', 'I am waiting for an appointment', 'I am waiting for my appeal'. These are the phrases in English showing the extent of the colonialisation of Home Office English into the structuring of the lives of people seeking sanctuary.

Other agencies and charities have to step in, and do so – but with rarely any meaningful resource for those seeking support as they lurch from project to project. I have seen letters appealing for financial hardship funds replied to by local authorities with a clear statement that there is real hardship and that this will entitle the appellant to £46 a year. I do not know how to live on £46 a year. Nor do people far more resourceful than myself. As I translate such letters, as I am often called upon to do by friends caught up in the system, we will make silent eye contact as the news sinks in. Then we will laugh and shake our heads. We know it is useless. We know life goes on, somehow. We are never quite sure how. Often in these moments there is a shrug of the shoulders and an appeal to God; to Jesus; to Allah; to Jehovah. The refuge of those with no material hope left.

If, ultimately, refugee status is granted, the waiting carries on: 'I am waiting for housing (again)', 'I am waiting for my national insurance number', 'I am waiting for my papers', 'I am waiting for my passport to be returned', 'I am waiting for a travel document', 'I am waiting for job centre', 'I am waiting for my benefits', 'I am waiting for ESOL', 'I am waiting for college', 'I am waiting to hear from my family', 'I am waiting to see my family', 'I am waiting for my wife/my husband/my children', 'I am waiting for appointment'. 'I am waiting for appointment' – I've lost count of how many times I have heard this, always without the use of the indefinite article, 'an', as if the indefiniteness of this 'an' is just too much effort to voice in a sentence.

Here, in this sub-Saharan transit city, no one has yet learned these words of Home Office English. Yet, waiting is who they are, their ontological state, it's how they spend their lives, and I join them in this rhythm of waiting. This UK economy of time wasted, waiting, of lives on hold, has its mirror image, here. It is one which finds an exact parallel in the lives of those either left behind 'back home' in Eritrea or, more often than not, stuck in limbo in one of the big cities where refugees take up residence. And it is present here, in this sub-Saharan city of waiters and whilers of time. For some it is indeed a life in refugee camps, but these are more the exceptions than the rule, and it is certainly the policy of the Office of the United Nations High Commissioner for Refugees (UNHCR) to use or construct refugee camps only when there is a 'crisis'. Integration – also known as the ability to live as normal a life as possible – is vital to minimising the damage done by the need to flee persecution most especially, as the flow of temporary visitors attests, when connections are lost or severed through displacement, and with the loss of all that had previously kept life safe.

Across the global South, lives are on hold. In the big cities of the South, the arrival cities for migrants and refugees, there is an economy of waiting, held in place by an economy of remittances. As in the UK, in many cities of the global South, those who have arrived can have little hope of work, will be subject to punitive and often punishing conditions, may be sold into or working in slave labour or entirely reliant on remittances from family in the global North, who might have gained refugee status, who send every penny back to those waiting in hope for a chance to start their own lives again.

These cities are also populated with those who have been deported from the North and whose claims failed despite the waiting processes. I clearly recall being taken around one such city in sub-Saharan Africa by a rickshaw driver who had spent six years in detention in the UK awaiting a decision, had eventually been deported, had been detained immediately upon arrival in Eritrea, his home country, tortured for two years for leaving the country and had eventually escaped and been able to find work in a neighbouring country, as a rickshaw driver. All the way through the journey, with a measured rage, he rained his scorn down upon the UK and its pretence at justice, its impotent system of decision-making and its wilful cruelty. 'I tell everyone who gets into my rickshaw', he said, 'everyone ... that the UK is rotten, it is a sham.'

In a perverted way this is indeed the much-vaunted policy of the UK's hostile environment working perfectly. Make life so dreadful that the stories that circulate will be shocking enough to deter people. It's got a deathly logic to it. But it doesn't work. What astounds me more, every time I spend time with the 'waiting peoples' of the global South, is the way the bonds of love and family are simply not to be deterred.

6 Waiting Brides

I am watching a wedding video, of a newly wed young woman now with child, who is part of the household here. I've been watching the video for the most part of the last couple of days. The majority of those watching the video with me, on this occasion, as on others, are either brides in waiting – those (engaged to be married) or the recently married. All are waiting alone alongside others in the same waiting situation. Their fiancées or spouses have returned to the country of refugee status to be sure that the protection will remain secure, or have work to return to, and, of course, important paperwork. Upon their return from the wedding they will file applications for family reunion for their new spouse.

Meanwhile, the wives or fiancées wait. Some wait and the child begins to grow within them. An application, if the money is there and travel can be secured with permits, medical tests and passports, might take eight or nine months if they are lucky. If the child comes beforehand, then another round of waiting begins, as new permits, medical tests and passports are needed, and DNA tests to prove paternity. I have known pregnant women granted travel rights who, on their due date, take a 10-hour flight, a 15-hour journey and all the indignity of country entry and border security for those who are black or non-native speakers of English just to avoid the continued torture of waiting. The medical injunctions not to travel do not override the determination to be as family, together, in the right place.

For the most part it's the elder sons who are sent overseas, or the young fathers. They are deemed fit enough for the arduous journey and will also be expected to find employment more quickly than daughters or young mothers. The young men come under heavy pressure to send money back home. Their families are stuck, waiting, in limbo; in contexts where employment is disallowed, subsistence depends entirely on remittances. Many young men end up in detention or asylum systems in Europe, where their claims are delayed for months, even years, and they often disappear from their families' lives, cutting contact during that time, as the shame of explaining their situation to waiting families is too hard. But money does eventually flow back to the 'waiting people', though often in fits and starts.

I've known of the pressure on money from friends in Glasgow with family 'back home'. They spend years longing to return for a visit, and those with refugee status are often eventually able to do so, once the expensive fares have been paid. But a visit also requires substantial resources, as the son or daughter returning will be expected to bring gifts (often good phones) and to pay for everything. The image of life in the West with trainers, clothes, perfumes, beauty products and technology is delivered in abundance to the waiting, watching consciousnesses of the global South. When governments and the media speak in terms of the old-fashioned and much discredited idea of push and pull factors of migration, they would do well to look at the aesthetics involved in the circulation of advertising and the images projected of a world of plenty onto the screens of those waiting in hope and expectation.

Waiting in the third country differs from the waiting in the asylum process, though it bears many affective similarities in terms of boredom and frustration and lingering doubts. What is perhaps most striking is the waiting of the young women. The apartments are full of the young people, the ones who have recently escaped conscription and are considering the next steps from the first arrival city. The quarter where we are staying is an immigrant quarter, full of Eritreans – the Ge'ez script mingling with the Arabic on every street and reminding me of immigrant quarters the world over – those entrepreneurial centres of economic generative activity born of need and necessity, of recently arrived people, needing those of their language, their family, their kith and kin, to translate the rules and customs of the new place, and provide for them the things of home – the clothing, the food, the cooking pots, the familiar household products with which to cook and clean, the home and the body.

Dealing with dirt in unfamiliar places is vital to staying well, and being able to rely on those things is a daily task and part of sustaining a people on the move, and a people waiting to move.

Those tasked with dealing with dirt are the women and the children, for the most part. Early in the morning, before it is too hot to move, the young women are busy brushing and mopping the floors, backs bent in the repeating actions of 'back home'. During the heat of the day we watch their wedding videos.

The three-day event that is a traditional and church wedding is filmed in its entirety and clearly the films are big business. They are all in Blen or Tigrinya. I understand nothing. Mostly there is singing of the traditional *mezmur*, the praise songs, which accompany celebrations. The videos are the proof of the marriage, of the money spent and the blessing of the family. They are the proof that the marriage has taken place according to the traditional forms. The videos focus on the bride's family, the negotiations between the male members of the families, and on the groom's place. Regularly there is the comment that the groom in the video is now 'in Canada', 'in Germany', 'in Sweden', 'in the UK', 'in Norway', 'in Australia'. Sometimes the grooms have reached these destinations over land, making the journey without papers. Sometimes, for the very lucky, and sometimes even after up to 30 years, their number had come up in the lottery run by the United Nations High Commissioner for Refugees/International Organization for Migration, and they were able to take the journey the safe way, with air tickets and passports and stamped paperwork.

For every man there is a story which involves border-crossing and then the sending of money back home for long enough for a marriage to be possible within the community. In a context where marriages are largely arranged, or semi-arranged, the brides are young women waiting to be in the right place at the right time, for an approach to come from a man's family, to her family, and for the groom-to-be to have the necessary status and income overseas, as demonstrated by the remittances sent back to the family both 'back home' and 'in waiting'. While young women do make the difficult journey, with false or no papers, and over treacherous seas, many more wait for the day to come when a marriage is possible, giving them a way of moving on from the country where they are stuck, to one where family can be made anew.

There is, of course, also the income threshold requirement in the host country; in the UK in 2018, for example, this was £18,700 year – an entirely unattainable figure for any newly arrived refugee working his way up the class pecking orders and taking his place after all of the unemployed graduates seeking a job with prospects of such a salary. A nurse's salary, for example, would be too little. I have encountered refugee young men working 90–100 hours a week in the UK in order to earn enough in their minimum-wage jobs, as drivers or in security or as carers, to be eligible to bring home their bride.

The determination to make a new home means great expense must be borne. For the bonds of marriage, there are dowry payments to be made, and a wedding to prepare, which will be captured on video over three days of celebrations and prepara-tions. There are relatives to fly into the third country – usually a country outwith the global North – perhaps Lebanon, or Turkey, or Kenya, or Sudan, or even Egypt or Ethiopia – countries which, with a visa and a sponsor, all members of the family will be able to enter.

To be able to attend a family wedding is such a simple thing. Many cannot, and the video serves as an important gathering point when, perhaps later, family members do receive permits, visas, passports, and can visit and watch the weddings to which they were invited, but could not travel. I ask, of the wedding I am watching, if various people I know in the family were able to attend. 'No, they are not allowed to travel from Norway for three years'; 'No, they do not have papers'; 'No, they are in detention'; 'No, they are waiting for their travel documents'.

There is a matter-of-factness to the responses. A closure in the way the sentences are spoken – blame on the tip of the tongue for those from the nations creating this emotional warfare on spirit, family, friend. But the words are not spoken. It is not personal, though it may feel tenderly so.

The waiting months and years for the brides and brides-to-be are languid times. There is nothing to do but keep a small, humble home clean and cooked-for in an immigrant quarter. It is not safe for us to go out on the streets during the daytime, as the soldiers patrol and there have been many roundings-up, detainings and sendings-back. A wariness accompanies the routines of the day. Whenever we venture out, we dress for the occasion, long yardages of cloth wrapped around waists, under arms, over shoulders and hair. We pass as far as possible in the dress that says we are integrated; we blend and belong. In the home, those who are older are served by the brides-to-be and new brides, or newly pregnant women. It is as if this is a practice for the keeping of home they expect will be their work when they make a new home, overseas. To do this task well may increase the chance of them moving on from the waiting state and into a state of migration. Their families will be pleased with their cleaning, their cooking, their diligent daily execution of the rituals of coffee and tea.

Alongside the household task of waiting there is a great deal of sleeping. 'We sleep long in the day and awake for the night.' It is cooler, and it is safer to live by night than by day. Between waking and afternoon sleeping, there is sweeping, then eating, then coffee. Between afternoon waking and night sleeping there is sweeping, then coffee, then eating. Over coffee there are conversations and wedding videos.

Coffee ceremonies take around three hours – with the beans roasted from their fresh, dried state, on a charcoal fire, from which incense will smoke, and the coffee served in rounds

and with an attention to detail – picking out the bad beans, carefully roasting on the fire, picking out burnt beans, grinding by hand, adding to the *gebana* – a clay coffee pot – and cooking multiple times on the coals.

It is the task of the new bride or bride-to-be to take on this ceremony, though it may be undertaken by other women. There is talk of absent family members,

of those who have travelled and visited, or where family are – spread randomly across the globe. And there is the viewing of many photos on phones. Talk is quite literally of what or of whom is in front of you, present, in the flesh or on a screen.

These are the things with which the waiting people order their existence. It is not that they have time for these things, but that this is what can be made when you have little but remittances to survive on. It's like a cruel sociological experiment where the question would be: 'If you took away people's right to live in their home country, and made them live somewhere where they have neither the right to work nor to move on, what will they do? How will they survive?' The answers are underground, behind the shutters and the many diaphanous curtains. To be sure, on occasion there are protests in the streets, mainly from locals protesting against the exorbitant price of bread. To be sure, one answer is that people are rounded up and sent back or detained routinely, and the bribe economy works well to release those who can raise the remittances in time. There is no other way to freedom. To be sure, people lie low – as we all do during my visit – making sure our paperwork is correctly registered with the police through the intermediary services, carefully avoiding check-points or areas where there are reports of soldier patrols from rickshaw drivers. We do not go out during daylight hours; when we do, we integrate fully, or as fully as possible. I purchase the clothing which will aid this, not so much for myself, but to be part of the camouflage for those with whom I am staying.

Some talk also of politics. Saudi Arabia, Dubai, South Sudan, Ethiopia, Egypt and occasionally Syria and Turkey, all feature in the discussion, interspersed with jokes about the political leaders, both 'back home' and in countries across East Africa. As I visit there are protests in the city and the Prime

Minister of Ethiopia resigns. Like wallpaper, Eri TV drones on in the background of the room, pumping out what we all know to be government propaganda, and into a room of knowing exiles, but providing enough of the backdrop of the familiar signs from home, of the singing and the celebrations and the stories for the military pomp and circumstances to be mildly tolerated. Though it does not go without plenty of comment.

7 Waiting Bodies

The family arrange for a woman to come and henna my hands and feet, and those of other women. Weddings and the celebration of reunions are part of the rhythm of the waiting life, and my own white skin and bodily presence are something of a canvas and novelty.

Henna-painting immobilises still further the already immobilised bodies. Something of a paradox, it is at the same time a way of celebrating mobilities – home-comings, travels, change and weddings. Those marked with henna when met on the streets will be known to have witnessed the possibility of mobility

in a world where borders are mainly closed. Henna, here, means movement, means a body has crossed or can truly hope to cross an international border. More than wearing the traditional dress, it is the henna on my hands and feet which draws strangers to me, more even than the colour of my skin, so luminous on the streets and yet, with henna, my linguistically mute body speaks loudly of a promise, a hope, perhaps of a marriage or a joyful reunion. It is through the henna that I return again to the proverb 'Gifts are in the feet'.

Time and again I remind myself that the waiting people are in reality displaced indigenous people. Here are cultures made new by refugees, ways of speaking, specific discourses about ways and laws and security forces and borders, and food prices, about marriages and crazy regimes the world over. Equally, there are specific cultural forms which arise under these conditions of waiting. But mostly what is practised, intensely, with more time at disposal, and more insistence given the threat, are the cultural forms which lived with the land 'back home' in Eritrea: the dress codes, the hair, the patterns on the skin, the gold sewn into the braids, the specific colours of the cloths for specific days; the way of giving thanks for food, the way of kissing a hand and bringing it up to the forehead in greeting; or the three kisses on the cheek in the morning, while bowing in reverence.

These bends of body are the natural order of things, living in exile, but are given heightened intensity by the conditions of waiting. To wait in exile is to attend to the language, the food, the greetings and habits of home; it is its own kind of sickness for home, and the waiting heightens the sickness and the time available for the practice of all that made for home, as carried in the body. The practice also deepens the habitus, deepens the body memory, drawing it into a fluency of rhythm which is anything but natural – or at least no more so than the playing of a full concerto by memory in the hands of a virtuoso. The waiting people are cultural, temporal, logistical and existential virtuosi. They have to be, for the alternative is homelessness. And to imagine one is not at home in this world is to cease to wait for that home to come, or to return.

Many comments are made, through touching my body, of changes to my hair, my body, my weight, my skin. The older women touch me in constant blessing. They sense my body being in transition: my greying hair, the lines on my face, the need for rest, the thinning of skin are all part of the way they attend to the fact that an older age is coming upon me; changing me for photos which will come up on family screens as those taken and shown from previous visits do, in years to come.

I arrive with dollars to cover the living expenses of between 5 and 20 waiting people during my stay, and watch as the cash is carefully counted out. A run to the local migrant market

means there will be plenty of traditional food – *injera* and sauce – for the one meal that day. Our waiting bodies need food.

Mostly we have a kind of porridge – *ghaat* – every morning, a thick baked flour and water dough covered in ghee and *berbere* spices and fresh yogurt, which you all eat together from a large bowl. It is filling and sustaining, and you don't need much to feel well fed. After this, there is one full meal a day during my stay. Usually this is either Eritrean or from the local culture; fresh bread is a treat and a bowl of spinach and piquant spices, the size of a large single-person portion of risotto in the West, feeds five of us for the main meal. How I eat and what I eat are a constant source of physical comment. I'm helped to eat with my right hand (I am a strong left-hander), so I spill sauce easily in my clumsiness. If I finish too soon, my body will be under scrutiny.

I can name all the dishes in Tigrinya, so as we sit on a rug on the floor around the common platter it's a time when I'm most able to participate linguistically. Gradually I'm able not just to use nouns but also sentences, proclaiming my enjoyment of what has been made. And join in the hand-washing and food blessings which open each meal. The repetitions mean that it is here, more than in any other activity, that I am achieving a little linguistic and habitual fluency.

Once the henna has finally dried, after around four hours, I am washed and dried and one of the older women in the family brings olive oil and massages my skin, my feet and hands. And then clothes are brought which will make me look Blen, the way the traditional brides look for their weddings, the way I should look to be a Blen mother. I obey, as my hair is plaited and veiled and I am given a scarlet dress, and silver coins for my braids. It takes time, and is moving. I'm close to tears as many women's hands attend to me, change me, and I feel myself risked again, for beauty and belonging of a very different kind to that of my own ways of dressing. It's clear that this is, yes, a pastime for those waiting; I am in a deep sense a play-thing just now. The dressing offers up my vulnerable body to more vulnerable bodies, for practices which all of us resist and decolonise. But it is also a ritual process, moving me into a form which is integrated in the family, which belongs, which looks right. Dressing someone new is, in many parts of this region, a way of making them belong. Waiting people with no home, displaced from their land, create belonging with cloth and henna and hands and hair.

8 Screens

Phones here do three main things:

(1) they keep you connected to the family you cannot see;
(2) they hold the photographs which are precious, at times car-
    nivalesque images of the life you and your scattered family
    lead;
(3) they show you the dangers in the routes out, the present
    and ever-changing pitfalls, the tragedies and possibilities of
    openings.

The connections to family are mainly via WhatsApp, because
it's the platform most resistant to bandwidth and reception
problems. Topped up from scratch cards and new sim cards
on a regular basis, the wifi is the lifeline. Without it the phones
themselves would be pointless. Those who focus on the phones
of migrants are missing the point, which is all in the connection,
the possibility of it. WhatsApp is a sign that the many resistances of technology and the many patient waitings for the signal
to return are repaid, in full, with signs of love from afar, signs of
safety for family, signs of life nearing again with a gift or a visit.
My phone, for the last 10 years, has been like the experience
of walking down the street in a village, with greetings, and an
asking after the family and wellbeing. When it's not possible to
do the social greetings face to face, WhatsApp is where those
seeking to connect remake their connections.

There is something about this new technology which makes
the waiting possible. Life and hope live through the working
connections, when the living connections have been broken and
the plugs pulled on ways of being which were previously taken
as given. When the 'internet is down', here, as in the whole of
the global North, the severing of connection to what is now

only to be held together electronically, from what was once held together in the taken-for-granted face-to-face rhythms of life, leads to a shudder of resignation as something of the precarity of the present penetrates consciousness more deeply. These moments of realisation also connect everyone in a room together in the same space of presence, rather than co-presence. And talk, I notice as I get the gist of names, turns to those with whom one would have been connecting, not constantly, but with a daily greeting or quick reassuring image.

There are various refugee young people around the world now who WhatsApp me every day, sometimes in English, sometimes in the language of the country where they now live, sometimes in their own language. It is a simple line I have come to expect during any and every day: 'Yes Alison, how are you?' 'I am well thank you, and you?' 'Yes, me too.' 'Selam Elsa, tak.' 'Selam kulum, Nkenyali.' 'Bonjour, comment ça va?' 'Tres bien merci, et toi?' And then maybe we will describe or send photos of ourselves and the weather, and sometimes the food – especially when it is celebratory cake. And that is all it takes. It's what Rowan Williams (2000) calls the necessary ceremonies that create the social bond. He speaks of these in the context of neighbours greeting each other over a hedge, but I have come to realise that the wifi connection, the virtual space, is the 'hedge' and that the greeting is vital to the social bond with those who have scattered. Life is now life online, and this is not a good thing or a bad thing, it's just a real thing, material, actually connecting.

When I sit with the family and speak of the things that matter and sustain my life, my own delights – my garden, my work with wool, music, beauty, cloth, performance, poetry and rhythms of prayer – then the photos on the phone, or the images on the ever-present TV screen, passing through in Turkish, Hindi, Tigrinya, Arabic and English – offer moments for inclusion. Gardens, flowers, henna tattoos or Blen costumes at celebrations mean someone will touch and say 'Elsa, Elsa' (it's easier than 'Alison' and it's becoming a name for me too) – and wave a limb or hand or tug my hair or my clothes and smile and say the few words we have learned around these things. Always words for what is good. Always words for what is beautiful. Always words, which are intended to bring smiles.

Sometimes I bring out my photo files on the laptop, or the laptop we brought and left here a few years back comes out and it's like the old-fashioned evenings I remember from childhood when mum and dad would do a family slide show. Carefully, one by one, the slides were loaded into a carousel (usually borrowed from my granddad) and we would look at wedding pictures, bridesmaids' dresses, christenings, gardening projects and holidays in the hills or by the sea, and children, always children covered in mud, or sand or chocolate pudding or any kind of amusing mess. It's no different here. I'm not making a universalist point, or, when considering difference, an essentialist one, but there is no doubt that both are co-present in the family times we are creating together through the bringing up of images around which we can cluster and laugh and remember and share.

As images slide by, often fleetingly, there will be one of someone – a lost love, an absent parent, or the family the one who is left behind is longing to see – and in the transitioning of the slides there is a quiet unease which settles and lifts momentarily. It's a moment of unspoken alliance in the commonly shared phrase across our social media platforms: 'I miss u'. We do the missing actively through the phones. I notice how in the quiet moments of looking at images, those waiting are also watching and returning to the celebrations and times of gathering which gave them hope. Like the photographs on the desks in offices, the phones show the specificities of the patterns of love and relationships. Up come pictures which I have shared via Facebook and I recognise how these too are connecting, electronic gifts which are like manna in the desert, food for a starving people, as they are to me too.

There is much written about co-creation, about establishing shared values in research, and much of it is good, worthy and in some cases even practical. I follow many of the tenets set by refugee groups about how they wish their ethics to be respected and about their desire for agency. They assume, rightly, asymmetrical relations of power, and yet in this situation, in this context, the asymmetries are more complicated. It is not that I am not rich, educated and experienced where the family, in absolute and in relative terms, are not, but it is that I am not the one in control. I am using the resources I have to hand – mainly my phone and my body – skin, cloth, digestion, movement, memories – to insert myself into a web of belonging. But I make none of the decisions about how the day is ordered, what might happen next and who will be responsible. It's not the kind of risk associated with cultural curiosity or professional ethnography, but rather that of a new family member, risking heart, because, really, in such matters of affect, we – I – can do no other. Onto-logical decreation. Decolonising the heart. And I have no words. No words. No right words. No words in Blen or Tigrinya.

At times – as I step into another rickshaw and remember all the risk-and-security-training advice about this being the single most dangerous thing I can do – I breathe deeply. I have put myself into a web of relationships here, where this is something about which I will have no easy choice. It would risk our safety to order an expensive taxi. It's often uncomfortable, and sometimes it's really humiliating: the reality of surrendering decision-making to others, of putting myself in a position where the mere notion that I might make a decision, be a decision maker, is simply ridiculous and unsafe for everyone – and everyone knows it. Especially me.

It can hurt like hell and I've come to realise that for de-colonising to happen, for space to be made for the kinds of creations, however simple and everyday they might be, where a different story that is not colonial can be told, this is how it will have to be. It is important that it is difficult. The difficulty with this difficulty is that, as researchers, and human beings, we are drawn to the tried-and-trusted, power-enhancing methods of working. These very methods then work against relationship and with control or dominating power. And here it is worth recalling Deleuze and Guattari's observation from 'On Wilhelm Reich' that 'the masses desired fascism', desired others to make the politics work, the trains run, the different people they had learned to blame for their ills go away (Deleuze & Guattari, 1983: 6). This is what has to be explained, and some of the answer is in the addictions to the comforts of the what is held in place by the colonial.

Decentring, decolonising, giving up power as control follow easily in contexts where we do not have linguistic control. The translanguaging happening here in this household is sufficient for us to move and create a life together in this space. The images we share on screen cement this affectively and in ways that move us towards one another and then apart, like the ebb and flow of the tide, built up now over many years.

This is perhaps most clearly visible as images flow by, or short videos are shared from social media, or what is happening in various places of safety or danger on potential routes ahead. For some branches of the family the road to safety in the global North came via the safe passage which is family reunion and the auspices of the International Organization for Migration (IOM). For this, the images are of tears of goodbye, but with gladness and hope, at departure airports and with flowers and hugs at arrival airports, and images of the first days in new open spaces – the greens of northern lakes, forests and gardens, the first meals together, the making of the food from 'back home' mixed with the food in the new home.

For others, the images are from the Sinai desert, Libyan beaches and even of boats sailing. There are common memes showing *mezmur*, the orthodox praise song and psalmody of lament accompanying pictures of rescue in the Mediterranean, and of soldiers and traffickers holding hostages for organ harvest. Images of desiccated bodies in the Sahara, of refugee camps where there is much disappearance to the east. And this time the new reality – there is always a new reality – news of slave auctions and of the initial deportations heralding the mass deportations from Israel. It's hard when I am asked what progress we have made on reunions ourselves, on the safe passages for the ones stuck, waiting with no hope of a rich enough UK bride to meet and love and marry. Here too I have no comfort, no words. Nothing money can buy.

Screens are important family members, as well as openings into lives lived online. Michael Cronin writes of this in *Translation in the Digital Age* (Cronin, 2013). This is not because they are just addictions, though there is this aspect, but mainly because they transport our loved ones into our midst, both past and present, in the making of images together, and co-present, and at the same time they show us shades within the narratives of our lives and those we imagine for our common futures. They are repositories for our changed narratives too. Here, the playful way my body becomes a carnival, a physical, overly coloured and designed presence which is to be photographed and stored as proof of the newness, of the different story which has been worked on, moulded and dressed in language and cloth in order to make it more familiar, to integrate it.

9 Parting Gifts

As the time comes for me to leave, my suitcase reappears in the room where we sleep and begins to be filled by the family. The cloths, a jug, some stands for the coffee pots, and then piles of dates, hibiscus tea and Sudanese popcorn. Gradually people arrive in my room as I pack the few clothes I had brought and give me things to take back for family in Scotland: soap, skin cream and the traditional spices, together, of course, with coffee beans, unroasted. Then the bread-baking begins and I am given fresh loaves. In my turn I delve into a case full of electronic cables and adapters for phones and good-quality second-hand children's clothes in abundance, together with gifts of small books of wisdom in simple English, for the elders, in honour of theirs. A bottle of perfume, some scarves and a tailored Habesha top all enter my case as gifts.

During the day, more and more ideas for gifts are generated. I am shown beautiful beading, made by a family member 'back home', and as I exclaim at its beauty I am asked if we would like this. Of course, the answer is yes. Any other response is unthinkable within the gift economy. I am viscerally aware that this part of our family not only feels, but is acutely, in our debt, and that weaving us into the fabric of family, through the presence of gifts in our home 'back home' from 'back home', is a vital symbol of our threads of connection.

It's a day of creativity and, although I could not anticipate it, as I cannot understand the snatches of conversation or am not present as ideas are discussed and people are remembered, all day long people come into my room with gifts for me or for other family members. It's like a long litany of remembrance of those I will see first, see soon. Each one is carefully packed for me into my case, and again and again I look, check and wonder at the economics of this. In so many ways, what I am transporting is worth perhaps less than £5 but fills a whole case. To transport it on an international flight seems counterintuitive at every level of the *oicos* – economically, in terms of the household and in ecological terms. But symbols defy the ordinary, everyday accounting logics, and their transportation will mean they grow in value, not least because in passing through my hands and across bodies in the company of a white woman, they also gain in value and in status. The story will be told of these everyday items, in the households, to many visitors, every day. 'These are the dates from the family in Sudan. They were brought by Elsa, by Alison, after she visited.' And then there will be the photographs, which accompany those already received 'back home' in Scotland, to the delighted exclamations of the family members there. These are the images of my hands and feet adorned with henna, telling of life, of rest, of transformation. The images already portend the arrival of goods, gifts. These are the hands for the task of carrying, the wrapping paper in human form for the presents.

As I pull up pictures accompanying previous visits, I realise how precious the recording and curating of family images have become. They begin to layer a story, which is indeed counterintuitive; they make tangible what has happened. They offer a way of retelling the story which has a newness and now is become a familiar part of family life. And there are the pictures too of the arrival at our home of suitcases and gifts after others have travelled, the wearing of new clothes, the opening up of teas and nuts and dates – always dates.

I have other images of suitcases in my home, reminders of sad times or just transition times. Suitcases from the times in detention; suitcases from the times of moving on – for many, as well as for family. There is something about the gifts and the cases which speaks particularly of the life in waiting and the life in exile. The cases move. The people do not. The gifts show that it is possible for substances to arrive intact. And perhaps for people too.

10 Muted and Hyphenated

During my stay, as I listen in hard to languages I barely can grasp, struggling to hold context and get the occasional gist as the words flow by in animated conversation, I knit. It's something I have done now for nearly 10 years when travelling or watching, and hearkening to the gist. It's a steadying craft and helps, too, with the boredom of not understanding or being able to participate.

As a teacher, public speaker and regular broadcaster and columnist, I am used to being given a great deal of airspace and to being listened to, pretty much anywhere I go now, professionally, worldwide. This is a remarkable thing, and it comes with great responsibility. I sit long with words and their crafting in my auditory imagination, and in the company of the words of those I will cite, so that I have lingered over their textual depths such that I feel ready to translate their meanings into my own forms of intellectual and creative understandings. I am used to being listened to attentively. I am used to my words being read and being taken seriously, not least by those making policies – and even, in some cases, by those who wield power.

To have a platform from which to speak as a teacher and as an understander of things, often of difficult things, is no small thing. In my work I try to share this space with those who are equally alert to and able to hold an audience but, by dint of their own migrations, have found themselves in contexts where their voices have not been heard, their accents have been shunned, their creative, skilful retelling of experiences in stories dismissed, their skin seen as too dark to suit the oh-so-white platforms of established power, except perhaps as a token embellishment.

In these spaces we work to interrupt my own confident, rehearsed and experienced voice with other destabilising tonalities. Guided by the way Brecht made his theatre – with interruptions which allow for a third voice, a critic or commentator, to challenge and disrupt – we work to move our audiences in a similar way. This is not the place for a full disquisition on the effects of this work – that's for another short book. But it's safe to say that the effects of the sharing are provocative, disturbing and disquieting, as well as being a small way of attempting to acknowledge the colonial potential of having gained a listenership, and distributing its potential across a more diverse spectrum, acoustically and visually.

I bend my head a little over my wool and needles. I'm making socks, to give away as gifts at the end of the stay, for 'Gifts are in the feet'. I am acutely aware of how, in this gathering, no one knows anything of me other than a muteness, a quiet, a body present to family but not able to speak. Occasionally someone will turn to me and explain what the content of the conversation has been. Sometimes I have indeed gathered the gist. I feel a relief when this is so. Mostly I dwell in a state of mild frustration and feel rather awkward, ungainly, deeply unattractive. So much of what is beautiful in what I make is in poetry, and here I am reduced to a few words for good. 'Tsubo, Tsubo', we repeat to each other again and again, and we feel an intense frustration together of wanting to know more of each other's spirit.

What am I missing? It's not that I'm really missing meaning – nuance, certainly, and the specific choices of words – but the meaning is caught in the objects, in the body gestures, the way the speaking body tells its story as the words embellish it. It's as if language comes from the body first, and the speaking is a song for the meaning in the body to dance to. 'Speech', says Merleau-Ponty, 'is a kind of singing in the world' (Merleau-Ponty, 2002: 193), and as I work through the phenomenology of muteness, and the gulf between this and my normal mode of being, there is much which appears and which cannot be known when we are in control of our speech and bodies. I too find myself expanding the gestures of my body.

Coda: Gifts Are in the Painted Feet

At the airport I do not need to do show my passport or worry about the languages I lack. I have learned words enough to bring me through, and my hands tell a story which advocates on my behalf. As I slide my passport onto the desk and use a word of greeting I have learned, there is interest in my hands, and gleeful, decolonised laughter at my speech. Questions are asked, slowly, carefully, in wonderment and with approval. I answer slowly, and with the languages I've learned. These are repeated by the listeners opposite. Words exchanged with colleagues who want to join in, some interpretation follows – this is after all, an airport. I show my hennaed feet and the response is warmer still. Soon you will have our passport, they say, approvingly, soon you will be one of us too.

Part 3: Decolonising the Multilingual Mind

With Piki Diamond, Chaz Doherty, Sophie Nock and Tawona Sitholé[1]

(1) My acknowledgements go beyond the normal conventions in this piece and rather than using a footnote to thank those who have helped, I instead choose to acknowledge those who co-authored this experience with me.

11 *Chitsva Chiri Mutsoka –* 'Gifts Are in the Feet'

Chitsva chiri mutsoka. I first learned these words from a Polish woman who shared them with me with such a brightness in her eyes, having just learned them from a Shona speaker who would later become both colleague and friend, guide and companion on the decolonising journey. 'It's all in this phrase; it's so beautiful', she said, and I can still hear her accent breaking open the English to let the air of her Polish English mix it into a far richer set of sounds. 'Gifts are in the feet', she says, laughing then slowing it down from a jig to an air, 'Gifts, are in the feet.'

Since learning the phrase I have returned to it on many an occasion. My Polish friend learned the phrase from Tawona Sitholé (Phipps & Sitholé, 2018), poet and playwright in residence with our Researching Multilingually at Borders and UNESCO projects. *Chitsva chiri mutsoka –* 'gifts are in the feet'. As the poem on page 16 reveals, I do not believe the proverb contains a whole truth; my own addition is from the harder learnings of decolonising journeys and encounters. But the partial truth is enough for the journey. It helps us keep our eyes on the land at our feet. Thinking with the gifts of the feet means we might concentrate on the stories, held by autochthonous peoples – by people of the soil – about the land, its holding and loss, as we move through it. Thinking with the gifts of the tears might mean our arrogant presumptions about the having, the holding and even the stewarding of land knowledge and language knowledge begin to be a recognition of the limits and the damage such ways have brought about, and enable a giving way and a making together of other ways of language learning.

In 2013 I spent six weeks in Aotearoa New Zealand as Distinguished Visiting Professor at the University of Waikato. A guest. Before it began, my spoken word (in the form of a plenary lecture) was received by a Māori scholar (in the form of a conversation) who had stayed in touch with me. Māori are the early inhabitants or indigenous peoples of Aotearoa and currently make up about 15% of the total population. Through her invitation I began an important new decolonising journey, which has since become vital for my developing practice and understanding of decolonising work in multilingualism. It is unique, as all subjective knowledge is, but it shares much in common with experiences and writings from scholars of feminism and postcolonialism (Irigaray, 2008).

The Land

'Tēnā koe Alison' – Greetings Alison – begins the email, sent at some implausible hour in the morning with a 13-hour time difference. A Māori friend is making some plans for 'entertaining' me during my extended stay in Aotearoa New Zealand. She is doing so with something of a twinkle in her eye and not a little mischief. 'I'd like to take you one weekend to the Whirinaki forest. I'm just seeing if I can time it that my mate is home so I could may be get some tā moko done and for you to meet the locals.' The forest is in the north-east of the North Island of Aotearoa, an area of rain forest and mountains. The landscape of Partick, Glasgow, gave way to new names and I found myself needing to reach for a dictionary to find out what it actually was she was going to get done.[1] Never one to turn down a trip to the forest I said yes, and a month or so later found myself driving with my friend along the road from Rotorua to Murupara, a small inland settlement, through thick mist, sulphur clouds and forest, increasingly convinced that the tree spirits were coming alive.

Due to the implausible number of roundabouts in Rotorua, it was almost midnight before we arrive at the old principal's house of the local school, on the *marae*,[2] slip off our shoes on the porch, and pad into her friend's house. Our host from the local tribe in the area is a Tūhoe Māori: a bushman, school teacher, hunter and extraordinary artist. The twinkle in the email from my friend glittered in his eyes. 'So, what do you do?', he said, and I was, as part of the moment of welcome, called to account for the use of my time. I always know it is good for me, a Pākehā – a 'fair skinned' person of European descent – to be in a minority. Several hundred years of exploitation, broken promises, ill-kept treaties, rape, robbery, oppression and greed crawl across my skin. There is a certain queasiness I have come to recognise among the Pākehā of conscience when it comes to Māori relations, one which comes from the knowledge of all that has been done, and done wrong, in our name. With the Tūhoe iwi – a particular tribe of the Māori – this is especially true, with conditions of acute oppression, violence, impoverishment and colonisation having dominated their history since the Pākehā settlers arrived. The queasiness is legitimate, as is the call to account. 'I work with refugees in Scotland', I say, and hear the English accent for its history of empire. Here is my ancestry standing face to face with someone else's, which has fought against the crown and Britain for their rights of land, dignity, life and language. The Tūhoe Māori are also warriors. There are hunting rifles propped up in the corners of the rooms and black power[3] artwork on the walls. My account for myself feels lame and inadequate.

He laughs, and we sit at his vast kitchen table with mugs of tea. His *moko* adds animation to the mischief and twinkle in his eyes. 'We called you Pākehā "refugees"', he says. 'When you all came on those boats they showed us pictures of the slums and houses in Glasgow you were leaving. You were refugees.' We begin a conversation which continues through my stay. It's not unlike being back home, at the Iona Community's centre at Camas, on the remote Isle of Mull – and indeed Camas and the deforestation of the Atlantic rainforest, the colonisation and clearance of the Gaels and their language, are my most present reference points as we share stories. He tells me of the settlement recently achieved with the government of Aotearoa and of the process now well under way to restore the land taken to the care of the Tūhoe Māori. He tells stories of how this was achieved. Stories of cunning and creativity, of suffering and servitude, of hope and of the need for decolonising the mind. I tell him of my time with refugees, of my time in Gaza and South Africa. These are political and human words between us. Words about land, struggle, hope, and where, in each of the situations – Gaeldom, Gaza, South Africa, Aotearoa New Zealand – I come from the line, country and empire that was a perpetrator.

We walk through the bush, checking traps, tasting peppery leaves, touching the bark and creepers, looking out to Ruapehu, the active volcano on the horizon, down the gun-sight on his rifle. I learn the names of trees, ridges, mountains, histories which he shares in an English filled out with Tūhoe Māori and not a little delight in beginning here, at home, on land which has been returned. In the workshop my friend is busy cutting out flowers for the stencils of mural artwork. They show me the *pounamu* – the greenstones from the river. It is *taonga* – treasure – and it reminds me of walking on the north shore of Iona, and stooping for pebbles – treasures too. Sitting in the sunshine with mugs of tea, bread and jam for breakfast looking out over the bush, forest and mountains he asks me if I would bring students here. 'This is a university.' There is so much work to be done, just in tackling the poverty, drugs and deprivation, and doing it according to Tūhoe ways: the care for the forest according to Tūhoe indigenous knowledges of the bush, the start of credit unions, of factories and exports with Tūhoe business values; the development of a highly disciplined, artistic school on the *marae*; his work as an artist to bring Tūhoe artistic practices into contemporary Tūhoe realities; work to renew the forest; work to live without the old enemy and then, perhaps one day, and in their own time, to make a peace with that past when something new has grown. There is nothing romantic about this work. It is a struggle, a struggle at the roots of the mind.

When it comes to the moment to leave and drive the long winding road back through the forest, he calls us together and says an incantation – *a karakia* – over us, in Te Reo Māori. I recognise some words now. Not many, but the ones I hear matter. They are the words which have kept this people alive, kept this bushman ahunting and agathering one, kept him turning to a fusion of graffiti art and tradition to paint murals with children in his school, kept him in negotiations with the crown to have the Treaty of Waitangi[4] upheld, kept him speaking the language of his ancestors and close to the spirits of *hapū*, *iwi*, of the *wharekai*, the gatherings of *hui* and *tangihanga*.[5] I hear the place names of the *marae*, the names of the places of this land, of *Te Urewera*, of *Ngāputahi*, of *Te Whāiti*, of *Whirinaki*. I hear other place names too and though my head is bowed as one at prayer, and my eyes closed, I feel his eyes on me in blessing and let the words he says cover my skin like *moko*. Is this reconciliation? Is this how it happens between us, as human beings? I crackle under the privilege and honour, the unconditional hospitality of this moment. I certainly know that it is not as simple as saying words, or even as a formal apology, such as those made through the settlements, by the crown. But I know that this is how perhaps we move from where we have been, to where we are, as yet, not.

'You have travelled and seen many things and many places', he says, after a pause and a little quiet and some movement, 'and no one knows about us here in the forest, but you know and you can tell of us'.

Aroha

My language skin
quivers.
You are making no sense
to me with
what you say.
But the ends of the
hairs on my arms
and neck, stretch to
meet you.
'Taonga' you say.
'Aroha.'
'Manaakitanga.'
I lean in
to your skin,
'korero'
not hand,
but face.
I lean in
to your breath
and become
air.

Alison Phipps, 2018

Aroha is loosely translated to love but in essence it is unconditional love.
Taonga refers to gifts and treasures.
Manaakitanga acknowledges your warmth and generosity. It often refers to one's hospitality.
Korero is a conversation, discussion, meeting or gathering.

In her 'Instructions for living a life', the poet Mary Oliver commands us to:

Pay attention.
Be astonished.
Tell about it.

For the queasy Pākehā of conscience, when it comes to Māori or any indigenous relations – and this is equally true for anthropologists today like myself – 'Telling about it' comes with the knowledge of what has been taken and done with knowledge in the name of greed. The queasiness and caution are not mistaken, are visceral and are important ways of knowing that we have also betrayed and been betrayed, that we are breakers and broken.

Yet here I am, commissioned, to 'Tell about it'. And as the anthropologist Ruth Behar says, importantly, I believe: 'Anthropology is nothing if it does not break your heart' (Behar, 1996: 177).

As the road winds back through the forest, before my friend falls asleep in the sunshine beside me and after calling in at Murupara for a necessary ice lolly, we speak quietly of these things. I share my discomfort at accounting for who I am. I tell of an odd feeling that it would be easier if there were settlers and colonists in my ancestry giving ground for an apology, or for guilt; I speak of the peculiarity of being English and spending nearly 20 years in Scotland. The history – both colonial and colonised – of that country in its quest for self-determination has changed and shaped me anew, and my politics, and how much more so after this encounter with Tūhoe. I think of the sadness in my English family and friends when I say I will be voting 'Yes' in the Scottish independence referendum, the sense of a new betrayal coming with what for me is a necessary part of the long, global process of decolonisation and living the apology. The queasiness of identity and politics and past remains and I wonder aloud with her, so enviably clear and proud and strong in her recovered Māori self, who my people are, and by what right, what right, what right, after so much betrayal, I too might be of a people, and of land.

In Andrew Grieg's *At the Loch of the Green Corrie* (2010), a book about keeping a promise to the poet Norman MacCaig, the narrator tells of his encounter with Somhairle MacGill-Eain (Sorley MacLean), who asked him: 'Who are your people?' The question has held me as it holds the narrator in the book. Sitting with my friend who has just shared her answer to this question through a weekend in the Whirinaki forest, with her people and their becoming, this question is even more acute. 'Perhaps you should write your *mihi*',[6] she says, 'your way'.

Notes

(1) *Moko* is a form of spiritual marking made by chiselling or drawing upon the skin.
(2) A *marae* is where Māori are able to practise their traditional ritual/cultural practices. It consists of a *wharenui* (meeting/sleeping house), a *whare kai* (dining room) and a *wharepaku* (ablution block).
(3) Black power art was associated with the direct-action liberation struggles of the 1960s in the United States and with the assassination of Malcolm X.
(4) Treaty document signed in 1840 by some of the indigenous population and the British crown.
(5) Translations: sub-tribe, tribe, dining house, gatherings and funerals which are practised on the *marae*.
(6) *Mihi* is a form of greeting which involves reciting ancestry, mountains, canoe, rivers, by way of introduction of the self.

12 *Mihi*

I was born in Sheffield, UK, a product of the new welfare state, to teachers. The hills I loved were Carl Wark, Higger Tor and Stanage Edge; the river flowed through Water-cum-Jolly Dale. In my genealogy there are no settlers that I can find, nor in my more immediate family – just farmers, butchers, weavers and the legacies of a dislocating modernity in the north of England. Grandma and Grandpa Blackburn took in strangers – the new immigrants brought from the Indian subcontinent to work the mills of Lancashire – and they took in refugees, escaping from the Prague Spring, and helped them find an occupation. Grandma and Grandpa Marham taught me to feed chickens, pigs and sheep, before feeding the village. I grew up in the cauldron of rage over Margaret Thatcher's destruction of the hope in my city as she closed the mines and the steelworks, and increased the rate of suicide in my school. I became a traveller – as a Roma woman selling clothes pegs at my door when my mother was carrying me, still unborn, said I would. My father taught me the names of the hills, flowers, trees and birds. My mother taught me to bake and to listen in hard to words. Music made me laugh and learn. Politics took root. I have never been to Soweto but it shaped the inner landscape of my youthful soul. Languages opened me out, anthropology worked to give structure to my thoughts, and theatre, liturgy and poetry gave them form.

Offenburg, Saint-Porchaire, Durham, Biberach, Clermont, Tübingen, Hayingen, Hornburg, Taizé, Balsall Heath.

I married Robert, and we took work in Scotland, in Glasgow – a city that was home from home. The hills became Beinn Sgritheall, Braeriach, Beinn a' Ghlò. I dangle my feet in the cold waters of the River Tilt and I swim in Martyrs Bay on the Isle of Iona. The University became my occupation and its books and teachings made me change my life, sent me back out into the world – a vessel for grief, a vulnerable observer, a witness of words, back to learn again the lessons of hospitality of my ancestors. I choked with shame at what has been done, by the crown, through history, in my name.

> Syria, Palestine, Gaza, South Africa, Malawi, Sudan, Ethiopia, Jamaica, Jordan, Egypt, Aboriginal Australia, indigenous Canada, Aotearoa New Zealand.

I read aloud the Freedom Charter from the Rivonia cell walls.

Everywhere land, stone and a meshwork of love and anger. With the years and struggles comes the love of silence and solitude. I have crossed Tongariro, climbed Mulanje, Skiddaw and Scafell Pike, worn out my shoes with walking and standing firm. I am English, Scottish, half Schwäbin and Blen. I became poet, gardener, lover, foster mother, bread-maker, piper, wool-worker and a person who prays.

My friend Piki took me to Te Urewera. I listened to the forest through the bushman, on the ridge. I slept deeply, bright with stars. I think there is now a *moko* in a corner of my soul.

'Tūhoe' may become my new word for Hope.

I am Alison.

Note

The text of Chapter 12 was first published in *Coracle* – the magazine of the Iona Community, an organisation and movement inspired by liberation theology. It was published under another name (Alison Swinfen) – one I sometimes use for publishing poetry. It was co-authored, in the sense noted here for Part 3 (see p. 74), with Chaz Tūhoe and Piki Diamond. I retain the copyright.

13 *Te Reo* – The Māori Language

O Te Tiriti o Waitangi, Te Papa,
Wellington, Aotearoa New
Zealand

This decolonising, multilingual subject – this Alison – returned in 2014 to the University of Waikato as a visiting professor. This time it was to staff cards, log-ins and a contract. One element of the contract was particularly important – the requirement that I, as a member of staff and public servant, would uphold Te Tiriti o Waitangi – the Treaty of Waitangi. Nothing if not a contested document, the Treaty is important as one of few legal documents recognising the ownership of lands and properties by Māori and also according them rights as British subjects. There are nine versions of the Treaty and not all *iwi* signed the document. While seen as a founding document of Aotearoa New Zealand, the sparseness of the text and the long history of the breaching of it by the colonisers have meant it has been an important source of activism and resistance, particularly since the 1970s.

Before I signed the contract of employment I asked Māori and Pākehā what a reasonable set of actions might be for me to show I was indeed actively respecting the Treaty. I was pointed to the work of Ranganui Walker and Mason Durie, together with work by Smith (Walker, 1983, 2004; Durie, 1998; Tuhiwai Smith, 2012). These are the decolonial Māori scholars of the years leading up to the crown apologies to Māori and of new settlements in Aotearoa under its bicultural policies and its renewed attempts to live under Te Tiriti o Waitangi. Inspired as they are by post-colonial thinkers such as Fanon (1965) and N'gugi Wa Thiong'o (1986), and connected to networks of indigenous scholarship, these authors offer a theoretical grounding and, through Smith in particular, a way of approaching both my practical dilemma of how personally I might best uphold and strengthen the Treaty, but also how it might be possible to use this thinking for a dual-track approach to decolonising multilingualism.

I resolved to use my time in Aotearoa to begin learning *te reo*, from the Māori Studies Department at Waikato. My request was something of a surprise to the lecturer I emailed, but nonetheless she took me on, and together we started on a journey which began, first and foremost, by decolonising my own cosmology, and my largely communicative, intercultural competency-based theories and practice of language pedagogy. Here are some examples of how.

Each class began with a *karakia*. This represented a prayer or invocation or incantation in *te reo* to the ancestors and the *atua* – the gods – to bring their blessing on the work, land, language, breath. We would pray these words together, slowly speaking them in step and reading them from a screen. The first task concerns the Māori cosmology and the connections with the lives of the ancestors and the gods. This, I learned, with not a little pride, is *whakawhanaungatanga* and would allow me to pronounce – not write – the *whakapapa*, my genealogy, my *mihi*. I entered a world of Ranginui, Papa-tūā-nuku, Tāne and – sky father, mother earth and the gods of life upon the earth and in the sky. I learned stories of the Māori understandings of creation and the way to shape my mouth around the vowels and learn to attempt, at least, to respect the pointings and accents. I learned that the pedagogy would not involve me making notes or writing down words but would be a learning according to Māori ways: *whakarongo* – to listen; *titiro* – to look; *korero* – to speak rooted in pedagogies derived from a privileging of meeting face to face; a gathering visual (*kite-ā-karu*), the aural (*rongo-ā-taringa*) and, importantly, the kinaesthetic (*mahi-ā-tinana*). Just from my experience of drama pedagogy the methodology made sense – the following of new actions with words and of new words with gestures.

The journey into *te reo* was a journey into a new respect for my own family. We spent much time learning about my own ancestors, their land, the ways they had lived. It was a languaging of the *mihi* I'd crafted after my time with Piki and the Tūhoe, but it was also what I can only describe fully as a spiritual experience, in the widest sense of this word, in that it brought me back in touch with the spirit of my childhood, with times spent with grandparents and parents, with my own daughter's life and the places where I had grown up and where I have migrated to myself. The dislocations of modernity took form in a strange, new language but also in a strange, new language pedagogy, and this defamiliarisation and making strange evoked the spirit of those I love – the living and the dead. Decolonising multilingualism became a spiritual act, a memorialisation, an experience of loss of land through my own family's displacement, and a revisiting of the ways in which the language of a new home – Scotland – had gently nestled into me and made itself at home in the movements and journeys of my body around the land. The language of the *karakia* – banished as it is from Western foreign language pedagogy – gained in appropriacy. The *karakia* added a humanising depth to what, in communicative language-learning contexts of Europe and North America, otherwise passes for a technicist acquisition of level, skill and competency.

After five weeks I was able to recite my own brief, protocol-informed *mihi* in *te reo* – introducing myself by way of my local river, mountain, mode of transportation, through my paternal and maternal ancestry, my partner and children.

> Te Whakapapa o Alison
> Tēnā koutou katoa e te whānau whānui
> Ngā mihi nui ki a koutou katoa i tēnei wā o te tau.
> Ko 'Calmac' tōku waka
> Ko Clyde tōku awa
> Ko Maunga Lomond tōku maunga tapu
> Ko Yorkshire-Scottish-Blen tōku iwi
> Ko Phipps-Swinfen-Andmariam tōku hapū
> Ko West End tōku marae
> I te taha o tōku papa ko Fred rāua Gertrude ōku tīpuna
> I te taha o tōku māmā ko Leonard rāua Annie ōku tīpuna.
> Ko Roy rāua ko Anne ōku mātua.
> Ko Rima taku tamāhine whāngai
> Nā reira, tēnā koutou, tēnā koutou, tēnā tātou katoa

After my final *te reo* lesson, reciting my *mihi*, we ended with a *karakia*. Repeatedly experiencing in my own body what happens with the turning into ceremony of what might otherwise have been a string of functional transactions has had a profoundly decolonising effect upon my own practice as researcher, learner and teacher. Reflecting on this need to suspend disbelief, to decentre myself, to work gesturally and privilege three of the senses – vision, hearing and touch – over the dominant privileging of text shifted the locus of my learning and has anchored *te reo* differently in my experience and recall. The attention, first, to cosmology and to the land and the spirits and gods means my journey through Aotearoa resonates with meanings, as every Māori place name forms itself into an acoustic shape ripe for pronunciation in my mind – 'wh' as 'f', the long flattened accent of 'ā' in 'Māori', humbling me each time, as I know I haven't yet got it.

It is perhaps this sense of humility that has been most important to the decolonising journey which lingers on my skin and in my gestures and with the tonalities of language, which relaxes as I return home, and then tightens again with each subsequent visit to Aotearoa. As familiarity grows, so does confidence in language, and with it comes, too, what must also be a proper humbling of position. The learning of languages which are not part of the canon of the European colonial legacies means being remitted to a place where the learning of *te reo* accompanies the necessarily slow, careful pace of the lifelong learning that is decolonisation.

While sections of this short book both relate to the de-colonising of what we might term body and heart, this work was very much experienced as a 'decolonising of the mind' (N'gugi Wa Thiong'o, 1986) through learning the language as an act of political and intercultural honour. 'Language, any language, has a dual character: it is both a means of communication and a carrier of culture' (N'gugi Wa Thiong'o, 1986: 13). Through beginning to learn *te reo*, according to ways which were alien to me as one versed in communicative language teaching and the pedagogies of the colonisers, and now of the globalisers, I was offering myself as a potential vessel, an intercultural holder and handler of words which are needing more space, more tending, than those of my own cultural tradition, for their survival or revival. I was offering a mind that could be, if for a moment, stripped bare of the words which give it global power, and the potential for ever greater theft, as N'gugi Wa Thiong'o describes it, and letting others choose how to teach me, how to decolonise my own mind.

Can You Hear My River?

'Can you hear my river?'
she asked, the sun
shafting through the old pine
trees, to catch the white
rapids and then refracting
into rainbows over the spray.

Can you hear how the sun plays
through this inexorable,
gravitational tumbling rush
over stones to the sea?
Can you hear the joy
when the sun plays with the
sound waves on this, she said,
the high bank,
of my own murmuring meander.

Can you hear its song?
Let me tell you it sounds like
Your own heart when echoing
round the inside of the calabash
you hold to your ear.

Can you hear my river?

It is wartime in summertime;
And for once the shallows have
appeared to reveal a point of crossing
and the sound is welcome,
gentle, not a roar of danger
and flood.

She kneels on the bank,
lowers her head to drink.
There is serenity
like that of this river
in the glitter of high
sunlight. It belies
stories of suffering,
told and telling,
which glisten
on her skin, and under the spell
of the river's chanting,
and the cold taste of nature on her lips,
are their own
intercedings for healing
and hearing
and a hearth.
It is only when standing
here that she can ask
you, in all serenity,

Can you hear my river?

Alison Phipps, 2018

The *koro*, the unfurling fern, is an image I suggest we pause with here. It is deeply of Aotearoa. It is experienced in the ways of learning *te reo* – Visual-kite-ā-karu; the Audio-Rongo-ā-taringa and the Kinaesthetic-Mahi-ā-tinana. To hear the language it speaks requires a listening in to seasons, and land, and straining beyond what we are accustomed to hearing. It takes us into the felt textures of pronunciation; it gradually unfurls itself, showing more and more of the strength of its roots, and the reach in each fragile frond. It's part of an ecology of speech and movement and growth and cycles of life. At times it is overshadowed by colonising species. At other times it breathes easy, if it is given space and protection.

14 Conclusions

Gifts Are in the Feet

The experiences described thus far have led to a series of reflections on the possibility or otherwise of decolonising practice for multilingualism.

Below are five key elements which this work leads me to claim are necessary for us to make a beginning.

(1) *Doing it*

If we are to find a way beyond the abstract impasse of postcolonial theory we have to move into Freirean praxis, and to do this we have to do it – to work to share the power of representation and presentation. To do this I – as a Principal Investigator, Professor, Research Leader with not inconsiderable cultural capital and a stake in the field – have to be the one to instigate the sharing. That is already a critical-essentialist move, and there is absolutely no way out of it. Just as with feminism we need men to cede places and we need to make new constellations, so with decolonising multilingualism – to enact this, then skin and language colour matters and has to be constellated, in the decolonising language pedagogy design, in such a way as to enable the possibility of such an enactment.

This is true at macro-, meso- and micro-levels. Without engagement and a sharing of power and the means of production with those who have been excluded from these means there can be no decolonising. So, language pedagogy and language policy need to keep asking themselves two questions. With whom are we to speak, in our new language(s)? And will this place limits on our normal ways of doing language pedagogy? If the answer to the first question means taking a look at communities round about us in cities and learning the languages of new arrivals, of refugees, or in remote areas learning languages of indigenous peoples and marginalised travellers, or visitors passing through, then this will indeed limit our normal ways of doing language pedagogy. It will expand the portfolio of languages and mean our work needs to be co-taught and co-learned. It will also require texts, such as this one, where the authors are given the kind of licence to blaze a trail and offer new routes to others who are still strongly bound by the requirements of academic publishing and engagement.

We cannot know if a decolonising multilinguality is creatable from between the historical subject positions which formed the colonial and postcolonial realities, unless we have a go at doing something, and critically thinking through and describing what the doing of this brings into being.

As intellectuals and artists we have to be able to look un-flinchingly into the hardest questions at the level of intimate, community and national speech, decolonising all that holds the too-powerful in place, living the discomfort of the double binds – all those which are still intact, experiencing their jagged-ness.

(2) *Knowingly mischievous*

To access the public money to do risk-taking work needs, I have come to believe, a certain amount of brass neck and mischief – clear-eyed and unapologetic. This has been part of a way of working which has developed in my collaborations with artists and indigenous peoples, those seeking refuge and asylum. It has come as something of a surprise in particular, around the very real nexus of the essentialised positions we are inter-pellated into (all of us) by dint of our skin, origins, experiences, language, class, journeys, positions.

During the early phase of the project, an indigenous colleague asked me to join him at a meeting with some funders of a project he was engaged in around the Commonwealth Games in Glasgow. We did not discuss the meeting beforehand; we let our different bodies, education, positions do the symbolic talking in the meeting and watched as our honest inhabiting of the positions into which the funders had interpolated us confounded those very positions and shifted the ground, meaning that new things could happen. We walked out of the meeting in silence, rode the elevator in silence, walked out onto the street together down the road together for a good five minutes side by side in silence – and then we began laughing. We knew exactly what had just happened, and what had been confounded, what mischief had been made and that it was necessary for the decolonising work we envisaged together.

Perforating, to use Agamben's phrase, the hardened assumptions that French, German, Spanish and maybe some Italian will continue to operate as world languages comes with conflict. With the acknowledgement by governments that skill in the language of a presumed enemy is needed by the state, as is also true for humanitarian aid, we see Arabic currently being interpellated into curricula by both such needs. What the previous languages symbolise is the persistence of European language hegemony and the working out of a curriculum rooted in the *Entente Cordiale*, in Europe at least. But this is not a decolonising move, and the work to queer the curriculum with a myriad of languages will be a work requiring artistry and mischief and a considerable amount of patient humour with the rigidly monolingual world.

(3) Representing the multilingual speaker.

The politics of languages sketched in (2) above means that not all languages are equal or equally validated. Breaking the politics of representation and presentation is a key challenge to decolonising multilingualism – not simply community schools or faith schools being able to teach 'their' languages but a collective engagement with languages other than those which might serve during a middle-class holiday in Tuscany or Provence. The languaged realities of the world when languages no longer remain rooted to specific territory but have broken loose and are establishing themselves in the life of new contexts and communities are an opportunity for decolonising work – readymade. We have people with languages we might learn who have, in many cases, come from the colonial contexts and from where the teaching of linguistic heritage enable precisely the kinds of redistribution of linguistic capital and power which decolonial language pedagogies will require.

(4) *Acoustics and kinaesthetics*

Spoken word and a consciousness of the work the body does to produce sound were key elements of my own learning of *te reo*, but also of the laughter-lessons and sharing which came in the work undertaken with Dangbe people, after the de-creation of my language, and my inability to dance on one foot. A decolonial multilinguality would be more like a dance than a panopticon. It would be learned standing, moving, walking and especially eating. Lessons would begin in music, as a song is easier for the vocal training of pronunciation than speech. A decolonial multilinguality would take to the streets and learn from many patient speakers; it would be part of a befriending, community practice, a purposeful consideration of how the world around us is shared in speech. This would not be easy at first. It would require intention as a key disciplining element of the learning, for guides would also be necessary – those who have worked in ground-breaking, decolonising, mischievous and creative ways before to see where a path may lead.

(5) *The spiritual/ritual/ceremonial dimensions*

Within Western, colonial models of foreign language pedagogy there is a learned secularism and queasiness about the ceremony, ritual and spiritual dimensions – a deliberate objective stance towards the world which is positivism's legacy. In my work in Aotearoa, with people seeking sanctuary, and at the hands of a healer, I have witnessed multilingual, cultural attempts to ground both the spiritual and the ceremonial in the general patterning of foreign language pedagogy. Working to cross that boundary into the subjective, affective, creative and ritual spaces which are necessary to the decolonising work is not accomplished all at once – indeed I'd go so far as to say 'always we begin again' – work for each dawn and dusk.

I'd go so far as to claim, with the many others who have made this point repeatedly, that we, in the West, cannot lead a way out of the colonial mess we find ourselves in. The normative assumptions about which languages may be taught, and the competitive attempts different languages will make – in the UK at present seen in Polish – to be accepted onto the life-raft of the language curriculum are simply more of the same, working to the same structural intent. The guides for us, leading the way out of this anthropological mess, will be those leading from below; from among the colonised, the willing artists and poets, together with those of contexts who are willing-to-be-guided and to learn anew, to embark on journeys of risk and mischief and discomfort and new pleasures; in short – to co-create new, multilingual ecologies of the postdecolony.

Disobedience

After letting my land rest,
I disobeyed.

I could do no other.

It began with a poem from the place of obedience.
The words made the clinging mist blush crimson
The bark in the forest burn red like cedar
Scented as richly and skelfing the skin.
The ink smudged,
the wax melted,
the carpet of leaves was moist.
The fish swam onto the hook,
onto the fire
and into the poem's wide,
wild mouth.

Alison Phipps, 2018

Titiro, Whakarongo ... korero.
Look, listen ... speak.

Chitsva chiri mutsoka
Gifts are in the feet.

References

Agamben, G. (1995) We refugees. *Symposium* 49 (2).

Arendt, H. (1943) *We Refugees.* In M. Robinson (ed.) *Altogether Elsewhere: Writers on Exile* (pp. 111–119). Boston, MA: Faber & Faber.

Behar, R. (1996) *The Vulnerable Observer: Anthropology That Breaks Your Heart.* Boston, MA: Beacon Press.

Bourdieu, P. (2000) *Pascalian Meditations.* Cambridge: Polity.

Buissink, N., Diamond, P., Hallas, J., Swann, J. and Acushla, D. (2017) Challenging a measured university from an indigenous perspective: Placing 'manaaki' at the heart of our professional development programme. *Higher Education Research and Development* 36 (3), 569–582.

Burgess, S.K. and Murray, S.J. (2006) *For More Than One Voice: Toward a Philosophy of Vocal Expression* [review]. *Philosophy and Rhetoric* 39 (2), 166–169.

Butler, J. (2005) *Giving an Account of Oneself.* New York: Fordham University Press.

Butler, J. (2009) *Frames of War: When Is Life Grievable.* London: Verso.

Butler, J., Zeynep, G. and Sabsay, L. (2016) *Vulnerability in Resistance.* Durham, NC: Duke University Press.

Cameron, D. (2013) The one, the many and the other: Representing multi- and mono-lingualism in post-9/11 verbal hygiene. *Critical Multilingualism Studies* 1 (2), 59–77.

Canagarajah, A.S. (1999) *Resisting Linguistic Imperialism in English Teaching.* Oxford: Oxford University Press.

Canagarajah, A.S. (2013) *Translingual Practice: Global Englishes and Cosmopolitan Relations.* London: Routledge.

Carson, A. (2006) *Decreation.* London: Penguin.

Cavarero, A. (2005) *For More Than One Voice: Towards a Philosophy of Vocal Pedagogy.* Palo Alto, CA: Stanford University Press.

Combs, M.C. (2014) 'Performing goofiness' in teacher education for emergent bilingual students. *Advances in Research on Teaching* 21, 287–312.

Costa, B. and Dewaele, J.-M. (2014) Psychotherapy across languages: Beliefs, attitudes and practices of monolingual and multilingual therapists with their multilingual patients. *Counselling and Psychotherapy Research* 14 (3), 235–244.

Blackledge, A. and Creese, A. (2010) *Multilingualism: A Critical Perspective*. London: Continuum.

Cronin, M. (2013) *Translation in the Digital Age*. London: Routledge.

Deleuze, G. and Guattari, F. (1983) *Anti-Oedipus: Capitalism and Schizophrenia*. London: Athlone.

Denzin, N.K., Lincoln, Y.S. and Smith, L.T. (eds) (2008) *Handbook of Critical and Indigenous Methodologies*. London, Sage.

Durie, M. (1998) *Te Mana, Te Kawanatanga: The Politics of Maori Self-Determination*. Oxford: Oxford University Press.

Fanon, F. (1965) *The Wretched of the Earth*. New York: Grove Press.

Freire, P. (1970) *Pedagogy of the Oppressed*. London: Penguin.

Freire, P. (2006) *Pedagogia do Oprimido*. Sao Paulo: Paz e Terra.

Geertz, C. (1973) *The Interpretation of Cultures*. London: Fontana.

Gramling, D. (2016) *The Invention of Monolingualism*. New York: Bloomsbury.

Heaney, S. (1995) *The Redress of Poetry*. London: Faber & Faber.

Irigaray, L. (2008) *Sharing the World*. London: Continuum.

Jones, A. and Jenkins, K. (2008) Rethinking collaboration: Working the indigene-colonizer hyphen. In N.K. Denzin, Y.S. Lincoln and L.T. Smith (eds) *Handbook of Critical and Indigenous Methodologies* (pp. 471–486). London: Sage.

Kramsch, C. (2009) *The Multilingual Subject*. Oxford: Oxford University Press.

Mbembé, J.-A. (2000) *De la postcolonie: essai sur l'imagination politique dans l'Afrique contemporaine*. Paris: Karthala Editions.

Merleau-Ponty, M. (2002) *Phenomenology of Perception*. London: Routledge.

Moore, R. (2015) From revolutionary monolingualism to reactionary multilingualism: Top-down discourses of linguistic diversity in Europe, 1794–present. *Language and Communication* 44, 19–30.

N'gugi Wa, T.O. (1986) *Decolonising the Mind: The Politics of Language in African Literature*. Kampala: East African Educational Publishers.

Nock, S. (2005) The teaching and learning of te reo Māori in a higher education context: Intensive fast track immersion versus gradual progressive language exposure. *Journal of Maori and Pacific Development* 6, 48–62.

Nock, S. and Crombie, W. (2009) Exploring synergies between Māori pedagogy and communicative language teaching. *Journal of Maori and Pacific Development* 10 (1), 17–28.

Oluo, I. (2018) *So You Want To Talk About Race*. New York: Hachette Books.

Phillipson, R. (1992) *Linguistic Imperialism*. Oxford: Blackwell.

Phipps, A. (2007) *Learning the Arts of Linguistic Survival: Languaging, Tourism, Life*. Clevedon: Channel View Publications.

Phipps, A. (2013) Linguistic incompetence: Giving an account of researching multilingually. *International Journal of Applied Linguistics* 23 (3), 329–341.

Phipps, A. (2014) 'They are bombing now': 'Intercultural dialogue' in times of conflict. *Language and Intercultural Communication* 14 (1), 1–17.

Phipps, A. and Sitholé, T. (2018) *The Warriors Who Do Not Fight*. Glasgow: Wild Goose Publications.

Ricoeur, P. (2007) *Reflections on the Just*. Chicago, IL: University of Chicago Press.

Scarry, E. (1985) *The Body in Pain: The Making and Unmaking of the World*. Oxford: Oxford University Press.

Skutnabb-Kangas, T. (2000) *Linguistic Genocide in Education – Or Worldwide Diversity and Human Rights?* Mahwah, NJ: Lawrence Erlbaum.

Spivak, G. (2012) *An Aesthetic Education in an Era of Globalization*. Cambridge, MA: Harvard University Press.

Te Urewera Board (2017) *Te Kawa o Te Urewera*. Available at http://www. ngaituhoe.iwi.nz/te-kawa-o-te-urewera (last accessed 29 May 2019).

Tuhiwai Smith, L. (2012) *Decolonizing Methodologies*. London: Zed Books.

Walker, R. (1983) *The Treaty of Waitangi*. Auckland: University of Auckland.

Walker, R. (2004) *Ka Whawhai Tonu Mātou – Struggle Without End*. Auckland: Penguin.

Weil, S. (2002) *Gravity and Grace*. London: Routledge.

Williams, R. (1977) *Marxism and Literature*. Oxford: Oxford University Press.

Williams, R. (2000) *Lost Icons: Reflections on Cultural Bereavement*. London: T. & T. Clark.

Williams, R. (2007) *Wrestling with Angels: Conversations in Modern Theology*. London: Eerdmans.

Index

acoustics, 92
African novels, 28
Agamben, G., 29
allies, 8
ancestors, 80, 84, 85
anthropology, 78
Aotearoa, New Zealand, 2, 14,
    74–9
    Māori language (Te Reo), 82–8
Arendt, H., 29
Aristotle, 26
Aroha (Phipps), 77
artists, 9
asylum seekers, 35
At the Loch of the Green Corrie
    (Grieg), 79
autoethnographic research, 39–40

bare life, 29
Behar, Ruth, 78
black power artwork, 75, 79n
brides, 49–55
Burgess, S.K., 27

Can You Hear My River?
    (Phipps), 86–7
Carson, Anne, 43
Cartesian dualism, 8–9
Caverero, Adriana, 26–7
ceremony, 84–5, 92–3
    coffee ceremonies, 53
change, 24
Chitsva chiri mutsoka see 'Gifts
    are in the feet'

co-conspirers, 8
co-conspiring work, 9
co-creation, 43, 62–3
coffee ceremonies, 53
colonial languages, 1
colonialism, 9–10, 15, 26–7
colonisation, 7–8
    see also decolonising multi-
    lingualism
Combs, Mary Carol, 9
control, 23–5
    see also power
cosmology, 84, 85
creative practice, 4
crisis of reception, 36–7
Cronin, Michael, 64
cultural codes, 57
cultural shift, 23

decision making, 63
decolonising multilingualism
    as changing of relationships,
        23–5, 26
    key elements, 89–93
    manifesto, 5–11
    willingness to, 28, 70
decolonising the heart, 44, 63
decolonising the mind, 28, 75,
    86
decreation, 43–4, 63
'Deep Play: Notes on a Balinese
    Cockfight' (Geertz), 22–3
Deleuze, G., 63
deportation, 48

destruction, 43
dialogue, 8–9
disalienation, 28
Disobedience (Phipps), 93
double bind, 5, 19, 20
dualism, 8–9
Dublin legal agreements, 35

English language pedagogy, 1–2
Eritrea
    cultural codes, 57
    languages, 42
    University of Asmara, 41
Eritrean refugees
    deportation, 48
    food, 58
    gifts, 66–7
    henna-painting, 56–7, 58–9
    hospitality, 34–6, 37–8
    phones, 60–1, 62, 64–5
    waiting, 49–55
experts by experience, 6

Fanon, F., 28
fern, 88
Folding a River (Phipps), 44–5
food, 58
For More Than One Voice
    (Caverero), 26–7
Freire, P., 6, 28
funding, 90–1

Geertz, Clifford, 22–3
gifts, 66–7
'Gifts are in the feet', 56, 69, 73
Gifts Are in the Feet (Phipps),
    16
gist, 39, 40, 42–3, 69
Gist, The (Phipps), 31
global North, 36–7
global South
    economy of waiting, 47
    migration, 36, 37
globalism, 9–10

Gravity and Grace (Weil), 13
Grieg, Andrew, 79
Guattari, F., 63

*Handbook of Critical and
    Indigenous Methodologies*
    (Denzin), 2
Heaney, Seamus, 13
heart, decolonising the, 44, 63
henna-painting, 56–7, 58–9
hierarchies, 23–5
    see also power
hospitality, 33–8
"hot-spot" metaphor, 36–7
hyphenated relationships, 24

If You Say My Name (Phipps),
    21–2
images *see* photographs
imperial languages, 1
income threshold, 52
'Instructions for living life'
    (Oliver), 78
integration, 47

Jenkins, Kuni, 24
Jones, Alison, 24

karakia, 84, 85
kinaesthetics, 92
koro (unfurling fern), 88

land, 14–15
localism, 9–10
logos, 26

Māori, 2, 14, 74–9
Māori language (Te Reo), 2, 14,
    76, 82–8
Māori scholars, 83
marae, 74, 79n
Mbembé, J.-A., 2–3, 26, 42, 43
Merleau-Ponty, M., 69
migration, 36, 37

mihi, 79, 79n, 80–1, 84–5
mind, decolonising the, 28, 75, 86
mobile phones, 60–1, 62, 64–5
moko, 74, 79n
multilingualism
    as colonial practice, 1
    see also decolonising multi-lingualism
Murray, S.J., 27
muteness, 69

New Zealand, 2, 14, 74–9
    Māori language (Te Reo), 82–8
N'gugi Wa Thiong'o, 1, 7, 28, 86
non-communication, struggle against, 40, 41

Obedience (Phipps), 12
Oliver, Mary, 78
Oluo, Ijeoma, 8
ontological decreation, 44, 63
otherness, 3

pain, 19–21, 25
Pākehā, 14
participant observation, 39–40, 42–3
phones, 60–1, 62, 64–5
photographs, 60, 61–2, 64–5, 67
poetic activists, 9
power, 23–5, 26, 62–3, 89
prayer (*karakia*), 84, 85
property, 7
public money, 90–1
public speaking, 68

reason, 26
reception crisis, 36–7
reconciliation, 77
Redress of Poetry, The (Heaney), 13

refugee camps, 36, 47
refugees, 29, 36–7
    language classes, 40
    New Zealand, 75
    waiting, 46–8
    see also Eritrean refugees
representation, 91
'Researching Multilingually at the Borders' project, 10–11, 29
Ricoeur, P., 40–1
rituals, 84–5, 92–3

Scarry, E., 20, 26
Scotland, 78
screens, 60–2, 64–5
Sitholé, Tawona, 73
Smith, Tuhiwai, 83
social bonds, 61
social media, 60–1, 62, 64–5
south–south migration, 36, 37
speech, 69
    see also spoken word
spirituality, 84–5, 92–3
Spivak, G., 5, 19
spoken word, 6–7, 9, 26, 69, 84–6, 92
    see also public speaking; voice
superorganisms, 22, 23, 24, 26, 27

Te Kawa o Te Urewera (Board), 14–15
Te Reo, 2, 14, 76, 82–8
'They are Bombing Now' (Phipps), 24–5
Tigrinya, 42
traditional healing, 19–21, 23–5
transindividuality, 9
translation, 40
Translation in the Digital Age (Cronin), 64

Treaty of Waitang, 76, 79n, 83
Tūhoe Māori, 74–9

ubuntu, 8–9, 11, 14
unfurling fern, 88
United Kingdom (UK)
    deportation, 48
    immigration decisions, 46–7
    income threshold, 52
University of Asmara, 41

voice, 26–7
    see also spoken word

waiting, 46–8
    brides, 49–55
    food, 58
    henna-painting, 56–7, 58–9
weddings, 49, 51, 52
Weil, Simone, 13, 43–4
WhatsApp, 60, 61
Whirinaki forest, 74–9
White Mask (Phipps), 25
Williams, Raymond, 4, 21
Williams, Rowan, 61

Xhosa, 9